9.12.18
6.1.19
24.12.20

Pocket
TENERIFE
TOP EXPERIENCES • LOCAL LIFE • MADE EASY

In This Book

QuickStart Guide

Your keys to understanding the island – we help you decide what to do and how to do it

Need to Know
Tips for a smooth trip

Regions
What's where

Explore Tenerife

The best things to see and do, region by region

Top Experiences
Make the most of your visit

Local Life
The insider's island

The Best of Tenerife

The island's highlights in handy lists to help you plan

Tenerife' Best...
The best experiences

Survival Guide

Tips and tricks for a seamless, hassle-free island experience

Getting Around
Travel like a local

Essential Information
Including where to stay

Our selection of the island's best places to eat, drink and experience:

◎ **Experiences**

✖ **Eating**

🍷 **Drinking**

✪ **Entertainment**

🔒 **Shopping**

These symbols give you the vital information for each listing:

☎	Telephone Numbers	👪	Family-Friendly
⊙	Opening Hours	🐾	Pet-Friendly
P	Parking	🚌	Bus
⊖	Nonsmoking	⛴	Ferry
@	Internet Access	Ⓜ	Metro
📶	Wi-Fi Access	**S**	Subway
🥗	Vegetarian Selection	🚊	Tram
📖	English-Language Menu	🚆	Train

Find each listing quickly on maps for each region:

Bar Hemingway

16 🍷 Map p233, B2

Legend has it that Hemi self, wielding a machine rate this timber-pan ered bar during showpiece is a en by Papa ar town. Dress s.com; Hôtel Rit ; ⊙6.30pm-2a

Lonely Planet's Tenerife

Lonely Planet Pocket Guides are designed to get you straight to the heart of a place.

Inside you'll find all the must-see sights, plus tips to make your visit to each one really memorable. We've split the island into easy-to-navigate regions and provided clear maps so you'll find your way around with ease. Our expert authors have searched out the best of the island: walks, food, nightlife and shopping, to name a few. Because you want to explore, our 'Local Life' pages will take you to some of the most exciting areas to experience the real Tenerife.

And of course you'll find all the practical tips you need for a smooth trip: itineraries for short visits, how to get around, and how much to tip the guy who serves you a drink at the end of a long day's exploration.

It's your guarantee of a really great experience.

Our Promise

You can trust our travel information because Lonely Planet authors visit the places we write about, each and every edition. We never accept freebies for positive coverage, so you can rely on us to tell it like it is.

The Best of Tenerife 125

Tenerife's Best ...

Survival Guide 143

QuickStart Guide

Welcome to Tenerife

Famed for its southern resorts (and not always in a good way), the joy of Tenerife is that it offers so much more than just another sun-flop on the beach. For a true taste of Tenerife, consider dramatic volcanic scenery, colourful colonial towns, world-class museums, sophisticated dining and earthy local bars where you'll still need Spanish to order a beer.

La Orotava (p76)
DESIREE MARTIN/AFP/GETTY IMAGES ©

Tenerife
Top Experiences

Parque Nacional del Teide (p116)

Awesome Pico del Teide (3718m) is the highest mountain in the Canary Islands, the highest mountain in Spain and, along with its extraordinary surrounding national park, will undoubtedly be the highlight of your trip to Tenerife.

CULTURA RM EXCLUSIVE/TIM E WHITE/GETTY IMAGES ©

GONZALO AZUMENDI/AGE FOTOSTOCK ©

Museo de la Naturaleza y el Hombre (p24)

This Santa Cruz museum has superb exhibits about Tenerife's natural history, plus archaeology, anthropology and fascinating informative displays about the indigenous Guanche population.

Tenerife Espacio de las Artes (TEA) (p26)

The edgy-industrial architecture of Santa Cruz de Tenerife's largest contemporary art space reflects the exhibitions, including works by Canarian Óscar Domínguez and an emphasis on social documentary and audiovisual presentations.

Museo de la Historia de Tenerife (p48)

La Laguna's historic centre is lined with 17th- and 18th-century ancestral mansions which, like the Museo de Historia, are distinctive for their colourful and decorative frontages.

Jardín Botánico (p62)

This lush botanical garden is home to plant varieties from all over the world and has an illustrious history. It is one of several magnificent gardens in Puerto de la Cruz.

Casa de los Balcones (p78)

This splendid example of La Orotava's mansions dates back to the 17th century and is a fine taster of this town's sumptuous colonial-style architecture.

Mercado de Nuestra Señora de África (p28)

This wonderful Santa Cruz market has history and atmosphere, as well as a great range of stalls selling everything from local banana wine to fragrant bunches of herbs and freshly baked bread.

Watersports (p92)

Forget the tidal wave of costly and contrived theme parks and head to the sea instead: the water's warm, the sun is (probably) shining and the watersports scene is awash with choice.

◯ Tenerife Local Life

Insider tips to help you find the real island

To really get under the skin of this island, take to the streets to experience such evocative and typically Tenerife delights as early-morning markets, chic shopping streets, shady squares and seafood as fresh as the morning's catch.

A Taste of Traditional Santa Cruz (p30)

▶ Old-fashioned stores
▶ Traditional dishes

Santa Cruz is a traditional working city. For travellers grown weary of souvenir tat and bland international fare, there are plenty of small family-owned shops to explore, and authentic spots to sample traditional Canarian cuisine.

Holy Candelaria (p44)

▶ Religious traditions
▶ Tapas trail

Visit this extraordinary coastal village over-shadowed by a mighty basilica and home to an intriguing combination of small shops, seafood restaurants and a steady stream of pilgrims.

Foodie La Laguna (p50)

▶ Gourmet markets
▶ Lively bars

Markets are an important part of daily life in La Laguna, just as bars are an important part of post-dusk partying. Experience them both over a long day (and night) out.

A Fishy Trail (p64)

▶ Fresh-off-the-Boat seafood
▶ Seaview terraces

A former fishing village, Puerto de la Cruz still retains a strong seafaring tradition with superb fresh seafood and an atmospheric harbour.

Timeless Tascas & Crafts (p80)

▶ Traditional craftsmanship
▶ *Tascas* (tapas bars)

Admire La Orotava's colonial-style buildings and traditional crafts (and *tascas*) untouched by time.

Backstreet Los Cristianos (p94)

▶ Local bars
▶ Independent shops

Los Cristianos' old fishing-village centre still has a *pueblo* atmosphere with its no-frills tapas bars and quirky independent shops.

Village Life in Garachico (p120)

▶ Tapas bars
▶ Local culture

In a village little changed by the passage of time,

CHRIS HEPBURN/GETTY IMAGES ©

Basílica de Nuestra Señora de Candelaria (p45)

Puerto de la Cruz (p60)

join the locals in the pretty main plaza before exploring the cobbled lanes and coastline, discovering convents, crafts and even a castle along the way.

Exploring the Anaga Mountains
(p122)

▶ Isolated hamlets
▶ Countryside hikes

A world away from the clamour of the coast, this mountainous region still has hidden corners to explore, as well as tiny *pueblos* (villages) with a handful of inhabitants and breathtaking views.

THE FISH WIFE, BY JULIO NIETO, TRAVELSTOCK44 - JUERGEN HELD/GETTY IMAGES ©

Other great places to experience the island like a local:

Playa de las Teresitas (p36)

Bodeguita Canaria (p36)

La Noria (p40)

Rastro (p43)

Guachinches (p71)

Bar Dinámico (p73)

Churrería Perdomo (p72)

El Médano (p93)

Kiosco San Telma (p113)

Las Galletas (p109)

Tenerife Day Planner

Day One

☀ Start your tour in the capital Santa Cruz with an early-morning breakfast at **Cafetería La Terraza** in the bustling and colourful **Mercado de Nuestra Señora de África** (p28). Follow this by a browse at the stalls, then learn about life many yesterdays ago at the nearby **Museo de la Naturaleza y el Hombre** (p24). Follow this with a stroll around the shops on **Calle Castillo** (p31) and the surrounding streets.

☀ Stop for a refreshing fresh fruit juice at **Bar Zumería Doña Papaya** (p40), followed by lunch at **Gom** (p39), known for its innovative Canarian cuisine. Continue to the lovely **Parque García Sanabria** (p34) and check out the sculptures and tropical plants. Then head back to the centre and hop on the tram to **La Laguna** (p46) for an afternoon of looking at the sumptuous colonial-style buildings and sights.

☾ When the time is right, swing by the gourmet market **Mercado de San Pablo** (p51), where you can graze on tapas and enjoy a tipple or two to get you in the mood for the clubs and bars in the vibrant student *barrio* (district) of **El Cuadrilátero** (p51).

Day Two

☀ Wake up early and head south to Puerto de la Cruz. Check out harbourside **Bar La Muelle** (p64) to join the fishermen for a traditional *tostada con aceite* (toast and olive oil) with coffee and fishing-boat views. Explore the centre and enjoy a mid-morning coffee and cake break at **Ebano Café** (p73) overlooking the picturesque church. Next, take a dip at the **Lago Martiánez** (p69), weather permitting, followed by a healthy light lunch at **El Limón** (p72).

☀ Next stop is the crowning garden glory of Puerto, the **Jardín Botánico** (p62). Carry on to the nearby beautiful colonial-style town of La Orotava and spend a couple of hours exploring the historic centre, including visits to the **Museo de las Alfombras** (p85) and the pretty **Jardínes del Marquesado de la Quinta Roja** (p83).

☾ Drop by **Casa de los Balcones** (p78) for a spot of early-evening souvenir shopping before dining at **Tascafe Grimaldi** (p88), set in the evocative 17th-century setting of the Casa Lercaro. Wind up your day by joining the locals for a nightcap at fashionable **La Tasca de Bullicio** (p88) with its creative cocktails and regular live music to keep you on your toes.

Short on time?
We've arranged Tenerife's must-sees into these day-by-day itineraries to make sure you see the very best of the city in the time you have available.

Day Three

☀ Start the day wandering the gracious streets of Garachico, on the island's northwest coast, joining the locals at the Plaza Libertad for a coffee at the central kiosk and gleaning a little about the town's history by visiting the **Convento de San Francisco** (p121) museum and the **Castillo de San Miguel** (p121). Enjoy a lunch of tapas at **Tasca de Vino** (p121) before heading for the fabulous moonscape of **El Teide** (p116) in the centre of the island, via the scenic TF-82.

☼ Stick your head high above the clouds in this stunning national park. The fit and fearless can return for an all-day hiking assault on El Teide's summit; the fearless but not so fit can take it easy in the cable-car ride to just below the summit. Everyone can enjoy the easy walk around the **Roques de García** (p117).

☾ Hit the road south heading for **Los Cristianos**. Head for the promenade here and a cocktail at the chilled-out **Beach House** (p100) followed by a seafood dinner at **Rincón del Marinero** (p97). It's been a busy day. Time for bed!

Day Four

☀ Head for the harbour in Los Cristianos and take a look at the kiosks advertising **watersports** (p92) and seafaring trips, including whale watching and deep-sea fishing. Make a decision for later in the day (or not), then have a hearty breakfast at **Sopa** (p98). Head for the old town and a peruse of the shops. Ditch the Kindle and pop into **Librería Barbara** (p100) for a browse through the excellent range of multilingual books.

☼ Enjoy a classically Spanish *menú del día* at **Restaurante Fortuna Nova** (p98) then hop on a bus to Playa de las Américas for an amble down the main, shop-flanked Avenida Rafael Puig Lluvina. Pop into the tourist office to see what's on then hit a sunbed on the sand at Playa de Troya.

☾ Catch an early show at **La Pirámide** (p114), then head to dinner at talk of the town, **The Oriental Monkey** (p109). There is no shortage of nightlife in this part of town ranging from sophisticated **Papagayo** (p112) to Irish pubs, live music and a more raucous choice of Brit-run bars.

Need to Know

For more information, see Survival Guide (p143)

Currency
Euro (€)

Language
Spanish (Castilian)

Visas
Generally not required for stays of up to 90 days (and not at all for members of EU or Schengen countries). Some nationalities need a Schengen visa.

Money
ATMs widely available. Credit cards accepted in most hotels, restaurants and shops.

Mobile Phones
Local SIM cards can be used in British/European and Australian phones. US and other travellers' phones need to be set to roaming.

Time
The Canary Islands are on Greenwich Mean Time (GMT/UTC), plus an hour in summer for daylight-saving time.

Plugs & Adaptors
Plugs have two round pins; electrical current is 220V/230V.

Tipping
Small change (€1 per person in restaurants) and rounding up (in taxis) is usually sufficient.

① Before You Go

Your Daily Budget

Budget less than €75
► *Hostal* or *pensión* doubles €35 to €45
► Three-course *menú del día* €7.50
► Plan sightseeing around 'free admission' times, generally on Sundays
► Markets for self-caterers

Midrange €75–€175
► Double room in midrange hotel €65 to €85
► Lunch in decent restaurant €15 to €25
► Use the excellent bus service, not taxis

Top End more than €175
► Double room in top-end hotel from €140
► Fine dining for lunch and dinner from €35

Useful Websites

► **Lonely Planet** (www.lonelyplanet.com/canary-islands) Destination information, hotel bookings, traveller forum and more.

► **Todo Tenerife** (www.todotenerife.es) Official tourism site with comprehensive information on all aspects of the island.

► **Reservas Parques Nacionales** (www.reservasparquesnacionales.es) The latest on climbing El Teide.

Advance Planning

Three months before Reserve your hotel early, especially in the southern resorts.

One month before Buy tickets online for a world-class performance at Santa Cruz de Tenerife's Auditorio de Tenerife.

One week before If you're planning to climb to El Teide's summit, you must reserve your place in advance. Allow a week, to be sure of a space.

❷ Arriving in Tenerife

There are two airports in Tenerife: Tenerife Sur (Reina Sofía; 📞922 75 95 10; www. aena.es), located 20km east of Playa de las Américas, and Tenerife Norte (Los Rodeos; 📞922 63 56 35; www.aena.es), located 11km west of Santa Cruz de Tenerife.

✈ From Tenerife Sur Airport

Destination	Best Transport
Costa Adeje	TITSA bus (111, 450)
Los Cristianos	TITSA bus (343, Express)
Puerto de la Cruz	TITSA bus (343, Express)
Santa Cruz de Tenerife	TITSA bus (107, 108)
Tenerife Norte	TITSA bus (343, Express)

✈ From Tenerife Norte Airport

Destination	Best Transport
Los Cristianos	TITSA bus (343, Express)
Puerto de la Cruz	TITSA bus (343, Express)
Santa Cruz de Tenerife	TITSA bus (102, 107, 108)
Tenerife Sur	TITSA bus (343, Express)

✈ At the Airport

Tenerife Sur Airport This airport receives the most traffic from tourists visiting the popular southern resorts. There are excellent airport facilities, including a tourist office, car hire, a VIP lounge, duty-free stores, gift shops and boutiques, as well as a pharmacy, newsagent, three bars-cum-restaurants and that all-important ice-cream stand. There are also several ATM machines and car-hire offices.

Tenerife Norte Airport The first airport to open on the island, Tenerife Norte caters to tourism to the north of the island as well as local business travellers. Facilities include a tourist-information desk, duty-free shop, pharmacy, car hire and ATM machines.

❸ Getting Around

Tenerife has an efficient and comprehensive public transport system, primarily comprising of a bus service that runs a spider's web of bus services all over the island, as well as within Santa Cruz and other towns. If you want to explore further afield, renting a car is highly recommended. If you'll be travelling a lot by public transport in Tenerife then it's worth investing in a Bon Via or Bono Bus card (www.titsa.com). Valid on all TITSA buses throughout the island as well as the city tram network, they give a 30% discount on standard fares as well as reduced entry to some tourist attractions. Cards cost from €7.50 (12 trips) to €45 (a monthly ticket for frequent users) and can be bought from any bus or tram station as well as some newspaper kiosks. Check the website for more details.

🚌 Bus

Tenerife has an impressive bus transport system that covers the whole island. Frequency, however, varies enormously from a regular service between major towns to a couple of runs a day for transporting workers and school children to/from the capital. Always check the TITSA (www.titsa.com) timetable carefully before you travel, especially at the weekends when most lines run a reduced service.

🚗 Car

All the big international car-rental companies are represented in Tenerife and there are plenty of local operators, as well. If you're staying for any length of time, consider reserving a car online in advance, especially with the smaller car firms,:they have a limited number of cars available, especially in peak seasons.

🚋 Tram

A convenient 12.5km (7.8 miles) tram (www. metrotenerife.com) links the main bus station in Santa Cruz de Tenerife with Avenida de la Trinidad in La Laguna.

Tenerife

Puerto de la Cruz (p60)

A gracious resort town with top-notch restaurants, tapas bars and nightlife, plus beaches for swimming and a leafy central plaza.

◉ Top Experience

Jardín Botánico

La Orotava (p76)

One of the prettiest towns on Tenerife, with great souvenir shopping and traditional restaurants and bars.

◉ Top Experience

Casa de los Balcones

Playa de las Américas & Costa Adeje (p102)

A buzzing nightlife and some of the island's top restaurants and hotels make this one of the most popular stretches of coastline for tourists.

Puerto de la Cruz

La Orotava

Parque Nacional del Teide

Costa Adeje

Playa de las Américas

Los Cristianos

La Laguna

Santa Cruz
de Tenerife

Santa Cruz de Tenerife (p22)

The Canarian capital in every sense with great shops, restaurants and sights.

◉ Top Experiences

Museo de la Naturaleza y el Hombre

Tenerife Espacio de las Artes (TEA)

Mercado de Nuestra Señora de África

La Laguna (p46)

A fascinating Unesco World Heritage town famed for its compelling historic architecture and sights, with a lively student-geared nightlife.

◉ Top Experience

Museo de la Historia de Tenerife

Los Cristianos (p90)

Superb beaches and lots of sights and activities for children make this one of Tenerife's top family destinations.

◉ Top Experience

Watersports

Worth a Trip

◉ Top Experience

Parque Nacional del Teide

Explore
Tenerife

Worth a Trip

Playa Jardín (p69) in Puerto de la Cruz
ATMAN VICTOR/GETTY IMAGES ©

Explore

Santa Cruz de Tenerife

The intrinsically Canarian capital of Tenerife combines a stately centre of historic buildings with lush subtropical parks and lively pedestrian-packed shopping streets. Terraced bars and restaurants plus elegant squares contribute to a leisurely atmosphere, while cultural highs are many – several of the island's top museums and art spaces are located here, along with an internationally acclaimed auditorium.

The Sights in a Day

At **Plaza España** (p30), pictured left, check out what's on at the tourist office, ponder the monument and have a paddle in the vast wading pool. Head up Calle Castillo for breakfast at **Palmelita** (p38), then stroll east to the **Museo de la Naturaleza y el Hombre** (p24) and/or the adjacent **Tenerife Espacio de las Artes (TEA)** (p26).

Kickstart your appetite by ducking into the **Mercado de Nuestra Señora de África** (p28) then lunch at **La Llave de Las Nubes** (p38). Stroll up Calle Imeldo Serís, taking a look at the **Teatro Guimerá** (p36) and adjacent **Centro de Arte La Recova** (p36), followed by a browse of the shops along Calle Castillo, then stride out to the **Auditorio de Tenerife** (p34).

After a cocktail at the auditorium's **Mag Café** (p40), hop on a bus to **Playa de las Teresitas** (p36) for sunset on the beach. Double back to town and head to the **Noria quarter** (p40). Cruise the tapas bars here or opt for a late dinner at **Bulan** (p38), which morphs into a bar at cocoa time.

For a local's day in Santa Cruz de Tenerife, see p30.

Top Experiences

Museo de la Naturaleza y el Hombre (p24)

Tenerife Espacio de las Artes (TEA) (p26)

Mercado de Nuestra Señora de África (p28)

Q Local Life

A Taste of Traditional Santa Cruz (p30)

♥ Best of Santa Cruz de Tenerife

Food

El Aguarde (p36)

Bodeguita Canaria (p36)

Tasca (p31)

Bars

Mojos y Mojitos (p40)

Barbas Bar (p40)

La Buena Vida (p40)

Getting There

🚌 **Bus** From Tenerife Norte airport, TITSA buses 102, 107 and 108 (€2.65, 20 minutes) go to Santa Cruz.

🚕 **Taxi** A taxi from Tenerife Norte airport to Plaza España will cost around €20.

Top Experiences
Museo de la Naturaleza y el Hombre

This brain-bending amalgam of natural science and archaeology is the city's number-one attraction and one of the best museums in all the Canary Islands. Set inside the aesthetically restored former civil hospital, exhibits are spread over three floors of well-lit galleries surrounding two courtyards. The island's flora, fauna and geology is covered in informative displays that chart the emergence of the island, plus there is a section on archaeology and ethnology, including a fascinating exhibit about the Guanches' lifestyle and culture.

👁 Map p32, D4

www.museosdetene rife.org

Calle Fuente Morales

adult/child €3/1.50

🕘9am-7pm Tue-Sun

Don't Miss

The Guanche People

The excellent exhibition on the indigenous population (2nd floor, area 1) includes a collection of prehistoric skulls neatly displayed in glass cases, along with tools, jewellery and everyday objects from daily life. There is a fascinating display of Guanche mummies and skulls with faces dried into contorted and grotesque expressions. Also look for the vertebrae pierced by a wooden spear. What a way to go...

Volcanoes

This exhibit on the ground floor (area 1) provides the perfect introduction to the archipelago with a giant panel noting the timescale of the islands, back to the formation of Fuerteventura 20 million years ago. There's also a complex display of how the islands were formed and vivid audiovisual displays that recreate the volcanic eruptions. Unlike much of the museum, most of the signage here is multilingual.

Vertebrates

Touch-sensitive screens provide access to fascinating information about the birds, mammals and reptiles found on the Canary Islands (1st floor, area 5). Listen to birdsong and discover which creature is now a threatened species, plus which are extinct – like the lava mouse and, more happily perhaps, the giant rat. Check out the giant lizard whose mummified remains are on display.

☑ Top Tips

▶ Most signage is in Spanish, however, there are multilingual information cards at each gallery's entrance.

▶ Avoid school groups by visiting at the weekend or late afternoon.

▶ Don't rush! There is a wealth of fascinating information here; allow at least two hours for your visit.

▶ Families note: there is a great playground next to the museum.

✖ Take a Break

The museum's classy courtyard **cafe** is obviously the best place to have a breather from all that academia, and serves a good selection of drinks, snacks and pastries. Once you've finished at the museum, head around the corner for a fresh fruit juice (or something stronger) at Mojos y Mojitos (p40), a fashionable bar with terrace seating on one of the city's most happening pedestrian streets.

Top Experiences
Tenerife Espacio de las Artes (TEA)

This extraordinary modern art museum has hugely contributed to Santa Cruz' importance as a cultural capital. The architecture of the dramatic modern building is cutting-edge contemporary, with three large light-filled galleries that create the perfect setting for exhibiting modern works of art and audiovisual displays by such surrealist A-listers as the Tenerife-born master Óscar Domínguez. There are also temporary exhibitions that typically include up-and-coming Spanish artists and photographers and reflect edgy contemporary themes.

◉ Map p32, C4

www.teatenerife.es

Avenida de San Sebastián 10

adult/child €7/free, film admission €4

◷ 10am-8pm Tue-Sun

Don't Miss

Modern Architecture

TEA's building is daring and contemporary and creates the perfect framework for the genre of contemporary art. The building was designed by the Pritzker Prize Laureates, Swiss architects Jacques Herzog and Pierre de Meuron, famed for their innovative construction, with a prestigious portfolio that includes London's Tate Modern. The dramatic triangular design combines concrete construction with vast windows, spacious sky-lit galleries, lofty greenery and dramatic contemporary lighting.

Óscar Domínguez

The museum's star exhibitor, Óscar Domínguez is considered the third greatest surrealist painter in Spain (after Joan Miró and Salvador Dalí). Born in La Laguna in 1906, Domínguez was a prominent member of the 20th-century contemporary Spanish art movement. His exhibits include examples of *decalcomanía*, an intriguing painting technique Domínguez created in which a mirrored pattern is created.

Biblioteca

The TEA's *biblioteca* looks more like the futuristic symposium space for a design company than a traditional library. This vast open-plan room with giant hanging globular lights, as well as plenty of natural light, angular lines and an overall sharp contemporary feel, also has 36 internet terminals that visitors can use, free of charge, as well as complimentary wi-fi. Plus, if you're foot sore, there are quiet cubicles where you can sit, read or have a snooze, and books and magazines for browsing, including some in English.

☑ **Top Tips**

▶ Take time to explore all the installations, including finding out what's on at the cinema.

▶ Parking is available across the street at the Mercado de Nuestra Señora de África.

▶ The galleries are not huge and you can often enjoy them solo if you visit early in the morning.

▶ There is no audioguide (yet), so make use of the free brochures available at the reception.

✕ **Take a Break**

The museum's **cafe** is generally buzzing with a clientele of students and art enthusiasts and is a great place for a caffeine fix, along with a homely slice of cake. Alternatively if it's post-noon, opt for a peach-flavoured mojito at La Buena Vida (p40) in the suitably arty *barrio* of La Noria.

Top Experiences
Mercado de Nuestra Señora de África

This is a tantalising market housed in an eye-catching building that combines a Latin American feel with Moorish-style arches and patios. A lofty clock-tower helps in locating the place – or just follow the shopping baskets; the *mercado* offers the freshest, competitively priced produce, and is the top choice for locals, including restaurateurs. Stalls are spread over two bustling floors and interspersed with colourful flower sellers, kiosks selling churros, benches for kickback time and lush subtropical greenery.

◉ Map p32, C4

www.la-recova.com

Avenida de San Sebastián

◷ 9am-2pm

Don't Miss

Specialty Stores

Save money by buying your gourmet deli items here, like jars of chilli-spiked *mojo* salsa, cactus marmalade, local honey, and herbs and spices. On the main Patio Naciente, head for stalls like Mi Mundo Gourmet, which sells and has tastings of cheese and *jamón* (ham); Herboristeria Mil Variedades, which specialises in medicinal herbs for every imaginable ailment; and La Pasta Fresca, which sells just that.

Architecture

The *mercado* was built in the early 1940s (look for the plaque near the rear entrance). This was a time when architects had abandoned *modernismo* and turned towards a more vernacular architectural style. Unlike traditional markets, stalls are organised around a flower-festooned central patio, which is a meeting-and-greeting place for locals and also used as a venue for concerts.

Local Wine

Look for **Canary Wine**, off Patio Naciente, where the charming owner will guide you through the local wines, including eco wines and the famous banana wine with the peeled-back price of just €8 a bottle. Another popular choice is *viña norte*, a Lambrusco-style rosé. Wine tasting takes place here on Sundays at 11am, advance reservations essential.

NITO/SHUTTERSTOCK ©

☑ Top Tips

▶ There's free parking underneath the market.

▶ Note that prices are set: this is not a market where you barter.

▶ Look for a stall selling fresh sugar-cane juice; it's often available mixed with rum.

▶ If you want to take photos of the stallholders, ask permission first and, better still, buy something from their stall.

▶ There's an excellent children's playground.

✗ Take a Break

Join the bleary-eyed stallholders at **Cafetería La Terraza** (☏ 620 12 67 10; Patio Naciente, Mercado de Nuestra Señora de África; mains €6-8; ⊙ 7.30am-3pm), here for their first caffeine fix of the day, and enjoy the early-morning market bustle at the adjacent fruit-and-vegetable stall. If it's later, head downstairs to the simple **kiosk** next to the seafood stalls and dine on some of the freshest catch in the city.

Local Life
A Taste of Traditional Santa Cruz

Given that Tenerife's capital is a typical Canarian working city, rather than a dedicated tourist destination, getting a taste of what makes Santa Cruz tick is essentially as easy as exploring the plazas and backstreets with their local bars, parks and family-owned shops. The following route should give you a head start.

❶ Plaza Príncipe de Asturias
Grab a coffee at the traditional **Kiosco Príncipe** (Plaza Príncipe de Asturias; ⏰8am-7pm Mon-Fri, to 3pm Sat) in this subtropical park, dating from the mid-1800s. Admire the award-winning sculpture *Courage* by Hanneke Beaumont, the traditional bandstand and fountain, and the lofty trees, including Indian laurels imported from Cuba. Always full of local strollers with plenty of bench space for gawping at folk.

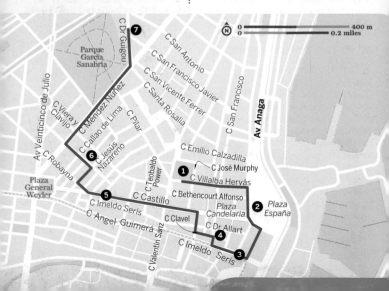

2 Plaza España

This emblematic plaza is at the heart of the city. Ponder on the memorial to locals who died during the Spanish Civil War, take a paddle in the vast wading pool, then duck down to the tiny underground **Castillo de San Cristóbal** (Plaza España; admission free; ⊙10am-6pm Mon & Wed-Fri, 11am-7pm Sat & Sun; P) to see fragments of the former castle that once sat majestically here.

3 Calle Imeldo Serís

Old-fashioned, family-owned shops and restaurants typify this historic city street. Stop by **El Guajiro** (Calle Imeldo Serís 15; ⊙10am-1.30pm & 5-7pm Mon-Fri, 10am-2pm Sat), which dates from 1953 and sells locally produced cigars (from €25 for 12). Even if you don't fancy buying any big puffers, take a look at the evocative interior, the walls papered with ancient photographs and yellowed newspaper cuttings.

4 Dining with History

Weave your way through the backstreets to **La Hierbita** (☎922 24 46 17; www.lahierbita.es; Calle Clavel 19; mains €10-15; ⊙noon-4pm & 7-11pm Tue-Sat, noon-4pm Mon). The first restaurant to be licensed here in 1893 in the (then) heart of the red-light district; dining rooms are spread over two creaky floors. Part of the building used to be a brothel, but there's nothing seedy about the excellent contemporary-style Canarian cuisine served here now.

5 Calle Castillo

The main pedestrian walkway in town is lined with shops and boutiques and is the city's top see-and-be-seen street for locals to promenade at weekends. All the national chains are here, as well as smaller independent shops. Just to the south of Calle Castillo's western end, you'll find **La Tienda de Aloe Vera** (☎922 24 36 01; Calle Imeldo Serís 96; ⊙10am-2pm & 5-8pm Mon-Fri, to 2pm Sat), which sells everything to do with this locally grown super succulent.

6 Soho

The nearby small grid of streets to the north of Calle Castillo is known as Soho and home to some of the most fashionable cafes, tapas bars and small independent shops. Time for a breather? Then head to **La Casita** (www.lacasitacafe.es; Calle Jesús Nazareno 14; mains €7-8, cakes €2.50; ⊙10am-midnight Tue-Sat; 🛜), managed by a young fashionable team but themed like grandma's country cottage. The cakes are sublime.

7 Canarian Cuisine

After a welcome respite sitting by the lily pond in the magnificent **Parque García Sanabria** (off Calle Méndez Núñez), head to nearby **Tasca** (Calle Dr Guigou 18; mains €6-10, menú del día €7; ⊙noon-3pm & 7-11pm Mon-Sat), one of the city's earthiest local restaurants, which makes no allowances for confused foreigners. The decor is plain, the queues are long and the food comes in huge portions comprising hearty old-fashioned Canarian classics.

ATLANTIC OCEAN

For reviews see

	Top Experiences	p24
	Experiences	p34
	Eating	p36
	Drinking	p40
	Entertainment	p41
	Shopping	p42

400 m
0.25 miles

Av José Primo de

Guimerá

C Bethencourt y Molina

C Fernández Navarro

C Buenos Aires

C Quevedo

C Garcilaso de la Vega

Av Tres de Mayo

C Fomento

Av Constitución

Recinto Ferial

Av Constitución

1 Auditorio de Tenerife

Parque Marítimo
5 César Manrique

4 Palmetum

Experiences

Auditorio de Tenerife
NOTABLE BUILDING

1 Map p32, C7

This magnificent, soaring white wave of an auditorium was designed by the internationally renowned Spanish architect Santiago Calatrava and possesses a Sydney Opera House-style presence, as well as superb acoustics. **Guided multilingual tours** (reserved in advance via the website) will take you behind the scenes of this remarkable building. ([📞]922 27 06 11; www.auditoriode-tenerife.com; Avenida Constitución; admission free; [🕐]guided tours 12.30pm Mon-Sat Oct-Jun, 12.30pm & 5.30pm Mon-Sat Jul-Sep; [P])

☑️ Top Tip

Sculpture City

In 1974, Santa Cruz hosted an international street-sculpture exhibition with leading works by such iconic masters of the art like Henry Moore, Joan Miró and Óscar Domínguez. Today you can enjoy these world-class sculptures while strolling around the city. Check at the tourist office for details on specific sculpture tours departing from the magnificent **Parque García Sanabria**, where several of the works are on permanent display.

Iglesia de Nuestra Señora de la Concepción
CHURCH

2 Map p32, D3

It's difficult to miss the striking bell tower of the city's oldest church, which also has traditional Mudéjar (Islamic-style) architecture) ceiling work. The present church was built in the 17th and 18th centuries, but the original building went up in 1498, just after the island was conquered. At the heart of the shimmering silver altar is the Santa Cruz de la Conquista (Holy Cross of the Conquest), which dates from 1494 and gives the city its name. (Plaza de la Iglesia; [🕐]9am-9pm Sun, mass 9am & 7.30pm)

Museo de Bellas Artes
ART

3 Map p32, C2

Founded in 1900 and formerly part of the adjacent church (note the fabulous stained glass), this excellent museum has an eclectic collection of paintings by mainly Spanish, Canarian and Flemish artists, including Ribera, Sorolla and Brueghel. There's also sculpture, including a Rodin, and temporary exhibitions. The massive battle scene canvases by Spanish painter Manuel Villegas Brieva are particularly sobering. Note that the galleries are accessed via several flights of stairs and that there is no elevator. (www.santacruzdetenerife.es; Plaza Príncipe de Asturias; admission free; [🕐]10am-8pm Mon-Fri, to 3pm Sat & Sun)

Auditorio de Tenerife

Palmetum

GARDENS

4 👁 Map p32, A8

Opened in 2013 on a former landfill area, this 12-hectare botanical garden has the most diverse collection of palm trees in Europe, imported from all over the world. A detailed mapped leaflet, as well as signage, helps in identifying the trees, . It's a peaceful place for a wander, with strategically placed benches for contemplating the seamless sea views. The central octagon is a shaded walled space with volcanic rock waterfalls designed to accommodate the more delicate species, including climbing palms from Yucatán. (www.palmetumsantacruz.com;

Avenida Constitución; adult/child €6/2.80, joint ticket with Parque Marítimo César Manrique adult/child €7.30/3.30; ⊙11am-1pm & 4-8pm Tue-Sun; **P**)

Q Local Life

Playa de las Teresitas

One of the loveliest beaches in Tenerife is just 6km northeast of Santa Cruz. Playa de las Teresitas has golden sand imported from the Sahara and is far more popular with (or rather known by) locals rather than tourists. The adjacent fishing village of San Andrés is good for an inexpensive seafood meal.

Parque Marítimo César Manrique
SWIMMING

5 ⊙ Map p32, A8

Located right off the city's main avenida is this park, where you can have a dip in one of the wonderful designer pools or collapse on a sunlounger and drink in the beautiful view and something refreshing at the same time. It's suitable for all ages, and great for children. (☎657 65 11 27; Avenida Constitución; adult/child €2.50/1.50, joint ticket with Palmetum adult/child €7.30/3.30; ⊙10am-7pm)

Museo Militar de Almeyda
MUSEUM

6 ⊙ Map p32, D1

Explains the military history of the islands and the successful defense of the city, brought alive by a superb 30m scale model of the flagship *Theseus*. The most famous item here, however, is *El Tigre* (The Tiger), the cannon that reputedly blew off Admiral Nelson's arm when he attacked Santa Cruz in 1797. (Calle San Isidro 1; admission free; ⊙10am-2pm Tue-Sat)

Centro de Arte La Recova
ART

7 ⊙ Map p32, C3

Located in a former market, this gallery houses temporary exhibitions of contemporary Canarian and mainland-Spanish artists. (www.santacruzdetenerife. es; Plaza Isla Madera; admission free; ⊙11am-1pm & 6-9pm Tue-Sat)

Teatro Guimerá
NOTABLE BUILDING

8 ⊙ Map p32, C3

One of the city's architectural highlights is the 19th-century Teatro Guimerá, fronted by a suitably theatrical giant mask sculpture. The sumptuous interior is reminiscent of Madrid's Teatro Real, with semi-circular balconied seating and plenty of gilt adornment. (www.teatroguimera.es; Plaza Isla Madera; ⊙11am-1pm & 6-8pm Tue-Fri)

Eating

El Aguarde
CONTEMPORARY CANARIAN €€€

9 ✗ Map p32, A1

Readers are raving about this special-occasion place that exudes a minimalist elegance to accompany the finely crafted dishes. The menu changes according to what is fresh in season, but includes a good selection of meat and fish dishes and at least one vegetarian choice. Desserts are exquisite; try the lemon

○ Local Life
Bodeguita Canaria

If you fancy trying traditional dishes like *ropa vieja* (literally 'old clothes'), a meat-based stew with chickpeas, head to **Bodeguita Canaria** (www.bodeguitacanaria.es; Calle Imeldo Serís 18; mains €8-10; ⊙1-4pm & 8-11.30pm Mon-Sat; 🖍), a local favourite with an earthy traditional atmosphere, chunky dark furniture and charmingly dated decor.

Understand
Arts & Culture

Architecture

There is really no such thing as typical Canarian architecture, as there have been so many different influences over the centuries and it is not uncommon for a building to reflect more than one architecture style. The colonial period is a good example of this architectural potpourri, typically reflecting elements from the Spanish, Portuguese, French, Italian and English architectural schools. Baroque influences are also in evidence, in particular in the beautiful carved wooden balconies and internal courtyards in the historic centres of La Orotava and La Laguna. Fast forward to the present and the late great César Manrique, whose ecologically sensitive creations are visible throughout the islands, including Tenerife.

Painting

Tenerife's earliest-known art forms date back to the cave paintings of the Guanches. The best loved sculpture from these times is the *Idolo de Tara*, a curvy feminine figure and Guanche idol, which you can see stamped on souvenir T-shirts and pottery. Among the best-known Tenerife artists is 17th-century Gaspar de Quevedo, impressionist Manuel González (1843–1909) and the famous local exponent of surrealism, Óscar Domínguez (1906–57), whose work you can see at several museums here including the TEA in Santa Cruz.

Crafts

Fine lacework and embroidered tablecloths, napkins and table linen can be found throughout the island and, although admittedly dated, they are exquisite, reflecting skills that have been handed down through generations. Beware of cheap Chinese imports (easily identifiable as they are far cheaper). Other popular items to weigh down your hand luggage include handwoven baskets, carpets and rugs.

Music

The symbol of the Canarios' musical heritage is the *timple*, a ukulele-style instrument of obscure origin, thought to have been introduced to the islands by Berber slaves in the 15th century. It's a small wooden, five-stringed instrument, which you will always see being played at traditional fiestas for dances such as the *isa* and *folía* and, if you're lucky, the *tajareste*, the only known dance to be passed down by the ancient Guanches.

mousse with cava and mint. (📞922 28 91 42; www.restauranteelaguardetenerife.es; Calle Costa y Grijalba 21; mains €15-25; ⏱1-4pm Mon-Sat, 9-11pm Tue-Sat; 🛜)

La Llave de Las Nubes

CANARIAN €

10 🍴 Map p32, D3

The folks behind this delightful small restaurant are passionate about food. Every morning they shop for the freshest produce at the market and create just a few choice dishes with a strong base in homestyle traditional cooking. The soups are particularly delectable – we recommend trying the watercress if it's available. It's always busy, so you may have to wait for a table (no reservations). (Calle Dr Allart 46; mains €7-10, menú del día €8; ⏱9am-5pm Mon-Fri)

✅ Top Tip

Carnaval

Channelling a true Carnaval spirit of exuberance and mayhem, Santa Cruz's own **Carnaval** (www.carnaval tenerife.com; ⏱Feb) is a nonstop 24-hour party-orgy. If you can time your visit to join in the fun, festivities kick off in early February and last about two weeks. Many of the gala performances and fancy-dress competitions take place in the Recinto Ferial (fairgrounds) but the streets, especially around Plaza España, become frenzied with good-natured dusk-to-dawn frivolity.

Palmelita

CAFE €

11 🍴 Map p32, C3

This charming cafe has a vintage exterior, a theme which continues within. Founded in the 1970s with German origins, the emphasis is on serious self indulgence: hot chocolate with double cream, or cold with vanilla ice cream; foamy frappes; buttery pastries and traditional German cakes. All of which are destined to put a contented waddle in your step. (📞922 29 11 07; www.palmelita.es; Calle Castillo 9; cakes €2.50-4; ⏱8am-8pm Mon-Sat; 👣)

Bulan

CONTEMPORARY CANARIAN €€

12 🍴 Map p32, C3

The interior here oozes atmosphere and history with original richly patterned tilework, wood-clad rooms and soft moody lighting. Go for such traditional Canarian dishes as cod cooked in a fresh tomato sauce with canary potatoes or the so-called Bulan Sword (skewer with chicken, pork and beef with mushrooms and courgettes). Morphs into a popular bar at cocoa time. (📞922 27 41 16; www.bulantenerife.com; Calle Antonio Domínguez Alfonso 35; mains €12-15; ⏱12.30pm-1am Sun-Wed, to 3am Thu-Sat; 🛜)

El Lateral 27

CANARIAN €€

13 🍴 Map p32, C2

Jovial staff, happy shoppers and a menu of tried-and-tested local dishes makes this place a perennial Santa Cruz favourite. Dishes like oxtail (or goat)

CANARYLUC/SHUTTERSTOCK ©

Carnaval

stew, sirloin in garlic sauce and seafood pie will not disappoint any large appetite. Veggie lovers should go elsewhere. (Calle Bethencourt Alfonso 27; mains €10-14; ⏰7.30am-midnight Mon-Sat; 👪)

Gom CONTEMPORARY CANARIAN €€

14 🍴 Map p32, C1

Part of the adjacent Hotel Taburiente, the modern menu at this sophisticated restaurant offers a creative take on otherwise typical Canarian and mainland fare. One of the more upmarket places in the city centre, it's popular with a slick business crowd at lunchtime. (📞922 27 60 58; Calle Dr Guigou 27; mains €10-15; ⏰1-4pm & 7-11pm; 🅿🛜)

Plaza 18 CONTEMPORARY CANARIAN €€

15 🍴 Map p32, D2

This fashionable place is located in one of the prettiest corners of the city, overlooking magnificent banyan trees and flower beds with the baroque Iglesia de San Francisco as a backdrop. The decor is colourfully chic and the cuisine hits the mark (most of the time). The menu includes risottos, gourmet burgers, salads and *tostas* (toast) with a variety of toppings, plus excellent local wines. (📞922 17 30 14; Plaza San Francisco; mains €11-16; ⏰noon-11pm Mon-Thu, to 1am Fri & Sat)

Drinking

Bar Zumería Doña Papaya
JUICE BAR

16 🍷 Map p32, B2

Delicious fresh fruit juices, including strawberry, mango, papaya, avocado and various delectable-sounding combinations. Local workers also come here at lunchtime for a quick and simple meal. (Calle Callao de Lima 3; juices €2-3.50; ☻9am-7pm Mon-Fri, to 3pm Sat)

🔍 Local Life
La Noria

The most fashionable drinking district in Santa Cruz is known as **La Noria**, which is, essentially, just one street: Calle Antonio Domínguez Alfonso, also confusingly known as Calle La Noria. The oldest street in town, it's named after the water mills that once stood here (*noria* is another word for wheel in Spanish); but was also a wealthy residential area at one time. Today pastel-hued historic mansions and houses have been transformed into cafes, restaurants and bars with sprawling terraces and an urban-chic vibe. Find it below the Puente Leones stone bridge, on the northern bank, opposite the the Tenerife Espacio de las Artes (TEA).

Barbas Bar
BAR

17 🍷 Map p32, D1

Yes guys, if you have a *barba* (beard) you will be made particularly welcome at this saloon-style bar across from the port. The emphasis is on imported beer, with a vast choice ranging from Crabbie's Original to Corona. Good atmosphere and occasional live music. (Calle Marina 9; ☻6pm-2am Mon-Sat)

La Buena Vida
BAR

18 🍷 Map p32, D3

Snag a table on the pavement overlooking the soul-stirring *iglesia* and order one of the moreish strawberry or peach mojitos – at just €3.50, they're a hiccup of a steal. A good place for interesting nibbles too, with hummus, grilled goat's cheese, and similar, available on the menu. (☏922 24 19 13; Calle Antonio Domínguez Alfonso 10; ☻noon-midnight)

Mojos y Mojitos
BAR

19 🍷 Map p32, C3

A laid-back place that serves decent food during the day, but at night morphs into a combination of cool cocktail bar and pulsating nightclub with DJs and occasional live music. (Calle Antonio Domínguez Alfonso 38; ☻noon-midnight Sun-Thu, to 4am Fri & Sat; 🛜)

Mag Café
CAFE

If you can't attend a concert or fit in a tour then, at the very least, you can glean some of the magnificence of the architecture of the Auditorio de

Mojos y Mojitos

Tenerife (see **1** 🎯 Map p32, C7), inside and out, by stopping here for a coffee or drink. The food, as in sandwiches and burgers, is more downmarket than you would expect in a setting such as this. (Auditorio de Tenerife, Avenida Constitucíon; snacks €3.50-5; 🕙9am-4.30pm Sun-Thu, to 7.30 Fri & Sat; 📶)

JL Murphy   IRISH PUB

20 🍺 Map p32, D3

This Irish pub has a chummy atmosphere and Guinness on tap, but is classier than many Irish imports. Live music most weekends. (Plaza de la Iglesia; 🕙5pm-2.30am Mon-Thu, to 3.30am Fri & Sat, 6.30pm-2.30am Sun; 📶)

Entertainment

Auditorio de Tenerife   LIVE MUSIC

Tenerife's leading entertainment option (see **1** 🎯 Map p32, C7) has dramatically designed curved-white concrete shells capped by a cresting, crashing wave of a roof. It covers and significantly enhances a 2-hectare oceanfront site. The auditorium hosts fantastic world-class opera, dance and classical-music performances, among others. (📞box office 902 31 73 27; www.auditoriodetenerife.com; Avenida Constitución; 📶)

JUERGEN RICHTER/LOOK-FOTO/GETTY IMAGES ©

PHILIP LANGE/SHUTTERSTOCK ©

Teatro Guimerá

Teatro Guimerá THEATRE

This fabulous art deco theatre (see 8 ⊙ Map p32, C3) is a popular venue for highbrow entertainment, whether music or theatre. (☏ box office 902 33 33 38; www.teatroguimera.es; Plaza Isla Madera; tickets €12-18; ⊙11am-1pm & 5-8pm)

Shopping

Dolores Promesas FASHION

21 🔒 Map p32, C2

This Spanish designer apparently became inspired as a child by the bolts of material, buttons and bows at her grandfather's modest haberdash-ery shop near Cádiz on the mainland. Her designs are aimed at various age groups and styles, ranging from casual printed T-shirts to fabulous floaty dresses in feather-light silks. (☏922 28 97 46; www.dolorespromesas.com; Calle Pilar 4; ⊙10am-2pm & 5-8pm Mon-Fri, 10am-1.30pm Sat)

Vintage Store 13 ANTIQUES

22 🔒 Map p32, D3

At first glance this shop resembles more of a jumble sale than anything else, but take the time to browse and you will discover all kinds of gems, including antique leather suitcases, kitsch ornaments and ceramics, denim

jackets and jeans, vintage postcards,
'60s floral frocks, silk scarves, records
and clunky retro costume jewellery.
(www.vintagestore13.com; Calle Dr Allart 32;
⊙noon-8pm Mon-Sat)

Carolina Boix   SHOES

23 🔒 Map p32, C3

Carolina Boix is a Tenerife-born and
-based shoe designer with shops
throughout the Canary Islands. Made
from synthetic fabrics, her inexpensive footwear (for men and women)
is renowned for its contemporary
comfortable style. (www.carolinaboix.com;
Calle Valentín Sanz 10; ⊙9.30am-8.30pm
Mon-Fri, 10am-8.30pm Sat)

La Isla Bookshop   BOOKS

24 🔒 Map p32, B2

This old-fashioned bookshop covers
four floors and has titles in English,
including novels, plus Canaries guidebooks and maps. (www.laislalibros.com;
Calle Imeldo Serís 75; ⊙9.30am-8pm Mon-Fri,
to 1.30pm Sat)

El Ganso   FASHION

25 🔒 Map p32, C3

This quality name in cool men's
fashion keeps trend-hungry stylistas
looking good. Think tweed jackets
with scarlet collars, military-style
tunic coats in sky blue and trainers

Local Life
Rastro

A vast rambling flea market (p43)
is held along two parallel streets
starting from Mercado de Nuestra
Señora de África and running along
José Manuel Guimerá to the coast
every Sunday from 9am to 3pm.
It's the usual mix, including pirated
CDs, cut-price underwear and
handmade jewellery, but is bustling
and fun and is always packed,
mainly with locals. Keep your
money out of sight.

with multi-coloured laces. Fashions
are funky, fun – and not for shrinking
violets. (www.elganso.com; Calle Castillo 19;
⊙10am-2pm & 5-8pm Mon-Fri, to 1.30pm Sat)

Dédalo   JEWELLERY

26 🔒 Map p32, C2

It may look like just another acces-
sory shop, but step inside to discover
well-displayed, exquisite jewellery
created by such eminent Spanish
and Canarian jewellers as Rosa
Mendéz, Carlos Reano and the shop's
namesake Dédalo. Don't miss Reano's
exquisite 'Bosques del Mar' series,
which combines resin, tropical woods
and bamboo with gold, silver and
bronze. (📞922 28 59 30; Calle Valentín
Sanz 14; ⊙9.30am-1.30pm & 5-7.30pm Mon-
Fri, to 1.30pm Sat)

Local Life
Holy Candelaria

Largely untouched by tourists despite being considered the holiest site in the Canary Islands, this small atmospheric town buzzes with life, particularly on Sundays. Narrow pedestrian streets are lined with little shops selling everything from kitsch religious items to more conventional souvenirs, while the traditional tapas bars and seafood restaurants are largely geared towards a discerning local clientele.

Getting There

Candelaria is located 19km south of Santa Cruz.

🚗 If you're driving, take exit 9 off the TF-1 motorway.

🚌 Several buses stop here, including the 111 and 115 (€2.35, 30 minutes).

❶ Coffee Stop

If you're arriving by bus head down to Plaza Teror via Avenida Condesa de Abona, stopping at earthy **Bar Mencey** (Avenida Condesa Santa María de Abona 1; snacks €2-3; ⏲6am-2am Tue-Sun) with its stamp-size interior, complete with TV and slot machines. Head to the outside terrace with its sea view across the way, and enjoy a strong coffee and *tostada con aceite* (toast with olive oil).

❷ Tapas Trail

Grab a map from the **tourist office** (☎922 50 04 25; Avenida Marítimo 176; ⏲9am-2pm & 4.30-7pm) and set off on one (or more!) of its five recommended Rutas de Tapas (tapas routes), to sample a variety of small dishes from various bars around town.

❸ Vino Time

Turn right on this pedestrian street and stop at **Maresía y Volcán** (Calle Obispo Pérez Cáceres 41; ⏲10am-2pm & 5-7pm Tue-Sun), a classy small deli selling local wines, cheeses and gourmet items, which also offers wine tasting and a reassuringly brief menu of tapas and *tostas* (toast with toppings), plus platters to share.

❹ Religious Souvenirs

Get into the soul-stirring mood by checking out the religious statues, photos, plaques and holograms of the Virgin Mary at **La Casa de las Imágenes** (www.lacasadelasimagenes.com; Calle Obispo Pérez Cáceres 17; ⏲10am-2pm & 5-7pm Tue-Sun), which claims to have the largest selection of religious imagery in Spain.

❺ The Basilica

Take a look at the grandiose **Basílica de Nuestra Señora de Candelaria** (⏲7.30am-1pm & 3-7.30pm Tue-Sun; P), which sits on a vast plaza and is home to the *Virgen de la Candelaria*, the patron saint of the Canaries. You can't miss the nine bronze, life-sized statues of the former Guanche Menceys who ruled over the island before the Spanish conquest. If your visit coincides with the official festivities for the Virgen on 15 August, you'll find the basilica's plaza filled with pilgrims and partygoers from all over the islands.

❻ Local Pottery

Take the right-hand steps up past the Basilica to the signposted **Centro Alferero de Candelaria** (www.candelaria. es; Calle Isla de La Gomera 17; admission free; ⏲9.30am-2pm & 5-7pm Mon-Sat), a small pottery museum where pots are handthrown, plus a shop where you buy the typical red pots, including the appealing *jarra de vino* (wine jug).

❼ A Fishy Lunch

Retrace your walk and follow the sea past the churros kiosks, playground, and small black beach, Playa el Pozo, until you reach the harbour and a giant Indian laurel tree generally shading a group of elderly card players. The seafood restaurant, **El Muelle** (Avenida Constitución 9; mains €8-12; ⏲8am-11pm Mon-Thu, to 2am Fri & Sat), serves that day's catch on a large terrace with harbour views.

Explore

La Laguna

Often overlooked by visitors to Tenerife, La Laguna is nevertheless one of the urban highlights of the Canary Islands, with sumptuous historical buildings washed in a paint palette of warm colours, lining poker-straight streets, together with fine shopping and dining options. Thanks to the university, there is also an overall youthful energy and possibly the island's most determined *marcha* (nightlife).

The Sights in a Day

☼ The best place to start is the tourist office, housed in an imposing 17th-century mansion, just to give you a taster. With map in hand, head next to the recently renovated **Catedral** (p53). For coffee and cake check out the well-named **Coffee Break** (p58), then squeeze in a couple of hours shopping on pedestrianised Calle Herradores.

☀ Enjoy a heartwarming lunch of traditional dishes at **La Casa de Oscar** (p55), before checking out the **Museo de la Historia de Tenerife** (p48) and surrounding historic mansions. Duck into the **Fundación Cristino de Vera** (p53), then stop for a vitamin-spiked fruit smoothie (and wifi) fix at **La Pera Limonera** (p58). Take a peek at the art gallery in the cloister-setting of the **Iglesia y ex-convento de San Agustín** (p54).

☾ Stride out to the Plaza Concepción and grab a chair on the square – and a glass of *vino* at **Casa Viña** (p57); climb the tower of the **Iglesia de Nuestra Señora de la Concepción** (p54) across the way, then head for dinner at cosy **El Tonique** (p57). Carry on to the nightlife hub of El Cuadrilátero and **Pub Gabbana** (p58) to gradually shift into high gear for a clubbing night out.

For a local's day in La Laguna, see p50.

Top Experiences

Museo de la Historia de Tenerife (p48)

🔍 Local Life

Foodie La Laguna (p50)

♥ Best of La Laguna

Historic Architecture

Catedral (p53)

Casa Lercaro (p48)

Casa de los Capitanes (p51)

Iglesia de Nuestra Señora de la Concepción (p54)

Cafes

Pastelería Diaz (p50)

Coffee Break (p58)

Bars

Casa Viña (p57)

Bar 7 Vies (p57)

Bar Benidorm (p58)

Getting There

🚊 **Tram** The most pleasant way of travelling from Santa Cruz. A one-way ticket also costs €1.35.

🚌 **Bus** From Santa Cruz, take TITSA buses 114 and 115 (€1.35, 20 minutes).

Top Experiences
Museo de la Historia de Tenerife

Founded in 1496, La Laguna was Tenerife's original capital and attracted wealthy merchants and noblemen who built their mansions here, many of which still line the narrow streets, their bright facades graced with wooden double doors, carved balconies, grey stone embellishments and elegant wood-shuttered windows concealing cool shady patios. One of the most emblematic *calles* (streets) is San Agustín, home to several magnificent buildings, including the 16th-century home of the excellent Museo de la Historia de Tenerife.

Casa Lercaro

⊙ Map p52, D2

www.museosdetenerife.org

Calle San Agustín 22

adult/child €3/1.50

⊙ 10am-8pm Tue-Sun

Casa Lercaro

Don't Miss

Museum Exhibits

The museum's latest acquisitions are two magnificent carriages, the French rococo 18th-century Berlin and the slightly later Landau (a carriage frequently mentioned in Jane Austen's novels). Other highlights include Guanche pottery and traditional crafts.

Casa Lercaro

For many people, the museum building is as fascinating as the exhibits. Dating from the late 16th century it was built by a family of Italian origin, hence such embellishments as the decorative floral lintels, typical of the Genoese Mannerism movement. The interior patio is magnificent, complete with *drago* (dragon) tree and a richly carved wooden gallery supported by stout stone columns.

Nearby: Behind-the-Scenes Tours

To see the historic La Laguna that's hidden behind heavy doors and walls, join a free guided tour (10.30am, noon and 4pm Monday to Friday, 10.30am and noon Saturday and Sunday) run by the tourist office. Tours are in Spanish, though can be arranged in English, German or French with 48-hours' notice. Tours include key historic sites, plus buildings that cannot be visited independently.

Nearby: Calle San Agustín

For the largest number of splendid mansions standing cheek to jowl, wander along the same street the museum is located on – Calle San Agustín. Look for the brass plaques outside the fancy facades; they have fascinating historical explanations about the buildings (in Spanish and English). Several of the buildings have been turned into offices, generally located around a grand central courtyard, which you can take a peek at.

☑ **Top Tips**

▸ Try and time your museum visit for a Friday and Saturday afternoon (between 4pm to 8pm) when there is free admission.

▸ Don't miss the superb gift shop at the museum.

▸ Parking is a nightmare. There's an underground paying carpark beneath Plaza San Cristóbal, but if possible come on public transport.

▸ Pick up the *San Cristóbal de la Laguná, World Heritage Site* brochure from the tourist office, it maps out La Laguna's architectural highlights, which are many.

✗ **Take a Break**

Grab an outside table at nearby Bar 7 Vies (p57) where you can enjoy traditional tapas, great coffee or a long cold *cerveza*. Alternatively, just around the corner, **El Encuentro** (Calle Viana 45; menú del día €6; ◷9am-8pm Tue-Sat, 10am-7pm Sun & Mon) has a great-value €6 daily menu.

Local Life
Foodie La Laguna

There's a lot to like about the local lifestyle in vibrant La Laguna. Combining the sumptuous sights, student buzz, a vigorous bar scene and a beguiling mix of traditional and gourmet restaurants (and markets), the town provides plenty of opportunity for visitors to get a taster of what makes the town tick.

1 Coffee & Pastry
Voted one of the top twenty patisseries in Spain by a national paper, the blaring TV and bright-orange decor at **Pastelería Diaz** (✆ 922 62 62 02; Calle Obispo Rey Redondo 6; snacks €2.50-5; ⊘ 8.30am-9pm Mon-Sat) may be a tad strident, but the pastries and coffees are superb, as attested by the inevitable queues at the door; try the custard-filled minicroissants.

2 Casa de los Capitanes

Make this magnificent 17th-century building your second stop. The **Casa de los Capitanes** (Calle Carrera 7; ☺9am-8pm Mon-Fri, to 2pm Sat & Sun) has a sumptuous inner patio. Home to regular exhibitions and the tourist office, find out what is going on, particularly any live music in El Cuadrilátero's myriad of bars.

3 Santa Clara Convent

Duck into the **Convento de Santa Clara** (cnr Calles Anchieta & Viana; adult/child €5/free; ☺10am-5pm Tue, Thu & Sat) to glean a little about the spiritual history of the town. There's a museum here with all kinds of priceless antiquities but the highlight is the audiovisual presentation about the history of the nuns and how exactly they arrived in La Laguna all those decades ago.

4 Mercado Municipal

Head to the colourful **Mercado Municipal** (Plaza San Francisco; ☺8.30am-3pm Mon-Sat) with close to 100 stalls, including fresh produce counters piled high with glistening fruit and veg, decorated by strings of garlic and bunches of fragrant herbs; this is also the place to buy the local smoked goat's cheese, fresh baked goods, flowers...and a canary in a cage (if you must).

5 Traditional Flavours

Immerse yourself in the local ambience at the time-worn **Bodegón Viana** (☏922 26 42 13; Calle Viana 35; mains €9-13; ☺9am-12.30am Tue-Sun; 🚻), which has changed very little since its founding in 1976 (the menu may well be the same as well...). Tuck into hearty portions of traditional Canarian dishes while catching up on the local soap on the corner TV.

6 Gourmet Market

The **Mercado de San Pablo** (www.mercadossanpablo.com; Calle Herradores 59; snacks €2-5, mains €9-15; ☺10am-11pm Mon-Wed, to midnight Thu, to 2am Fri & Sat, 1-9pm Sun; 🛜) is the latest hotspot in town for a pre-night-out tipple accompanied by gourmet tapas and a live jazz duo. Or stop by earlier in the day and make a meal of it. Cross continents with Cuban to Indian and Japanese delicacies.

7 El Cuadrilátero

Seize the night by the scruff and join the students who head to this rectangle of vibrant bars and clubs northeast of the university. At its heart, pedestrianised Plaza Zurita is simply two parallel lines of bars, clubs and pubs, so there's no shortage of quaffing choice. Choose between chilled-out bars, whimsical drinking dens and sweaty dance-til-you-drop venues.

0   250 m
0   0.1 miles

C Quintín Benito

Plaza San Francisco

C Tabares de Cala

C Cabrera Pinto

🚍 17

C Lucas Vega

C Anchieta

C Rodríguez Moure

C Santiago Cuadrado

9 ❌

C Viana

C Nava y Grimón

C Herradores

3 ⊚

14 ⊚ Plaza Concepción

Iglesia de Nuestra Señora de la Concepción

20 🔒

21 4 ⊚
C San Agustín

Iglesia y ex-convento de San Agustín

Museo de la Historia de Tenerife

C Capitán Brotóns

12 ❌

C Obispo Rey Redondo

8 ❌

15 ❌

C Juan de Vera

16 ❌

2 ⊚⊚
Fundación Cristino de Vera

13 ⊚

C Herradores

19 ❌

Catedral

1 ⊚

C Manuel de Ossuna

7 ❌

C Carrera (C Carrera)

C Bencomo

C de Higuera

C San Juan

22 🔒

6 ❌

C Deán Palahí

Convento de Santa Catalina

5 ⊚ Plaza Adelantado

C José C Llarena

C Juego

🛈

C del Consistorio

C Santo Domingo

C Baltasar Núñez

C Pablo Iglesias

C Barcelona

11 ❌

Av Trinidad

C Catedral

10 ❌

Plaza San Cristóbal

C Padre Herrer

C Molinos de Agua

Av Calvo Sotelo

C Morales

C Heraclio Sánchez

C Dr. Zamenhof

18 🍺

C Doctor Antonio González

Museo de la Ciencia el Cosmos (850m)

EL CUADRILÁTARO

For reviews see

⊚	Top Experiences	p48
⊚	Experiences	p53
❌	Eating	p54
🍺	Drinking	p57
🔒	Shopping	p58

ZM_PHOTO/SHUTTERSTOCK ©

Catedral

Experiences

Catedral CATHEDRAL

1 ⊙ Map p52, C3

This cathedral was completely rebuilt in 1913. A fine baroque retable in the chapel is dedicated to the Virgen de los Remedios and dates from the 16th century. Other highlights include some impressive paintings by Cristóbal Hernández de Quintana, one of the islands' premier 18th-century artists, and a splendid Carrara marble pulpit carved by Genovese sculptor, Pasquale Bocciardo in 1762. (www.catedraldelalaguna.blogspot.com.es; Plaza Catedral; ⊘8am-6pm Mon-Sat, to 2pm Sun)

Fundación Cristino de Vera ART

2 ⊙ Map p52, D2

La Laguna's prime arts venue houses a mixture of top-calibre temporary exhibitions as well as a permanent collection of works by acclaimed contemporary artist Cristino de Vera, who was born in Santa Cruz de Tenerife in 1931. There is also a thought-provoking audiovisual presentation about the artist and his work which is subtitled in English. (www.fundacion cristinodevera.com; Calle San Agustín 18; adult/child €3/free; ⊘11am-2pm & 5-8pm Mon-Fri, 10am-2pm Sat)

Iglesia de Nuestra Señora de la Concepción
CHURCH

3 ◉ Map p52, B2

Constructed in 1502, one of the island's earliest churches has subsequently undergone many changes. Elements of Gothic and plateresque styles can still be distinguished and the finely wrought wooden Mudéjar (Islamic-style architecture) ceilings are a delight. Take a look at the font where apparently (any remaining) Guanches were traditionally baptised, then climb the five-storey tower for stunning views of the town and beyond. (Plaza Concepción; tower €2; ⊗8.30am-1.30pm & 6-7.30pm Mon-Fri, to 8.30pm Sat, 7.30am-2pm & 4.30-8pm Sun)

Iglesia y ex-convento de San Agustín
CHURCH

4 ◉ Map p52, C2

This ruined church is out of bounds, but you can peer through the gap in the wall at the cactuses and other plants busy reclaiming the building's structure. The cloisters, filled with tropical plants and flowers, which are open to the public, are probably the prettiest in town. The rooms surrounding the cloisters contain an art gallery of frequently changing local works. (Calle San Agustín; ⊗10am-8pm Tue-Fri, to 3pm Sat & Sun)

Convento de Santa Catalina
CONVENT

5 ◉ Map p52, D3

The closed order in this convent are still active. On 15 February each year the remarkably well preserved body of Sister María de Jesús de León Delgado, who died in 1731, is rather ghoulishly put on display. The convent also contains a small religious museum. (Plaza Adelantado; adult/child €3/free; ⊗10am-5pm)

Eating

Guaydil
CONTEMPORARY CANARIAN €€

6 ✗ Map p52, C3

You can't go wrong at this delightful contemporary restaurant with its punchy, playful decor. Dishes are deftly executed, exquisitely presented and sensibly priced. If

---

Q Local Life

Science Museum

If you enjoy pushing buttons and musing on the forces of nature, you can have fun at the excellent **Museo de la Ciencia y el Cosmos** (☏922 31 52 65; www.museosdetenerife.org; Calle Vía Láctea; adult/child/student €5/ free/€3.50, planetarium €1; ⊗9am-7pm Tue-Sun; P), which introduces key scientific concepts in an engaging and thought-provoking way. Located 1.5km south of Plaza Adelantado and easily accessible by the tram to Santa Cruz (which stops right outside), it also has a planetarium, so you can stargaze during the day.

you are ordering a salad, which we recommend, ask for a half portion as they are huge (staff won't object). Other typical dishes include oriental couscous, prawn-stuffed crêpes and an irresistible Cuban mojito sorbet. (www.restauranteguayadil.com; Calle Dean Palahí 26; mains €8-14; ☉1.30-4.40pm & 8-11.30pm Mon-Sat; 🛜)

La Casa de Oscar
CANARIAN €

7 ✖️ 🍴 Map p52, C3

This place always has a great buzz, particularly at weekends when the tables are packed with exuberant local families tucking into dishes like grilled tuna in a coriander-spiked sauce, spicy sausage omelette or grilled meats with *mojo* (spicy sauce). Lighter appetites can snag a barrel table and fill up fast on the Galician-style *pintxos* (tapas) that line the front bar. (📞922 26 52 14; Calle Herradores 66; mains €8-10, pintxos €1.80; ☉8am-midnight)

Tasca La Carpintería
SPANISH €€

8 ✖️ 🍴 Map p52, B2

You may have to blink a few times if you're coming in from the sunlight, as the dining room is dimly lit with dark burgundy walls. The menu errs on the traditional side and is resolutely meaty with good wholesome dishes like *ropa vieja* (chickpea-and-pork stew) and braised ribs. Desserts are not all out of a freezer, thankfully, and

Iglesia de Nuestra Señora de la Concepción

include freshly made fruit pies. (📞922 26 30 56; www.tascalacarpinteria.es; Calle Núñez de la Peña 14; mains €12-15; ☉1-5pm & 8pm-midnight Mon-Sat, 1-4pm Sun)

Tasca 61
ORGANIC €

9 ✖️ 🍴 Map p52, D2

Organic, locally sourced produce and a Slow Food-philosophy are the hallmarks of this tiny place with its limited but delicious menu of daily specials. Even the beer is locally crafted at the only eco-brewery in Tenerife: Tierra de Perros. (Calle Viana 61; mains €7-9; ☉12.30-3.30pm & 7.30-10.30pm Wed-Fri, 7.30-10.30pm Sat & Sun)

Understand

Food & Drink

Don't confuse the traditional culinary fare here with that of the Spanish mainland; there are distinctive differences with dishes reflecting Latin American and Arabic influences, with more spices, including cumin, paprika and dried chillies, than the Spanish norm. Like the mainland, however, social eating and drinking is central to the Tenerife lifestyle.

The staple product here is *gofio*, toasted grain that takes the place of bread and can be mixed with almonds and figs to make sweets. The traditional *cabra* (goat) and *cabrito* (kid) remain the staple animal protein. The rich, gamey *conejo en salmorejo* (rabbit in a marinade based on bay leaves, garlic and wine) is common, as well as stews (*potaje*, *rancho canario* or *puchero*) of meat and vegetables simmered to savoury perfection. Fish is also a winner, with the renowned horse mackerel (*chicharros*) of Santa Cruz de Tenerife even lending their name to the city's residents: the *chicharreros*.

Also recommended is the *sancocho canario*, a salted-fish dish with *mojo* (a spicy salsa based on garlic and red chilli peppers). This sauce is the most obvious contribution to the Canarian table, and is typically served with *papas arrugadas* (wrinkly potatoes; small new potatoes boiled and salted in their skins). The most typical dessert is *bienmesabe* (literally 'tastes good to me'), a mixture of honey, almond, egg yolks and rum.

Cafe culture is part of life here. Locals like their coffee strong and bitter, then made drinkable with thick sweetened condensed milk. They are not big tea drinkers and if you have a preference it may be wise to pack your own teabags, although there are a couple of speciality shops that sell a wide range.

Tenerife is the principal source of wine and the red Tacoronte Acentejo was the first Canarian wine to earn the grade of DO *(Denominación de Origen)*. If you are a beer drinker, stick to the excellent La Dorada, a very smooth number brewed in Santa Cruz de Tenerife. The island is also home to the organic craft brewery Tierra de Perros, which is available at some eco-style restaurants and health stores.

Tapasté
VEGETARIAN €

10 ✖️ Map p52, D4

If you have a burger beast of a partner, bring them here to taste the delicious vegetarian variety, prepared several different ways with toppings like hummus and *almogrote* (spicy cheese). Plus Tapasté are not too pious to scrimp on desserts; try the chocolate tart with a berry topping. Appropriate pared-down decor: look for the lettuce-green painted doors. (📞822 01 55 28; www.tapaste.es; Plaza San Cristóbal 37; mains €8-12; ⏱1-4pm Mon-Sat)

El Tonique
CANARIAN €

11 ✖️ Map p52, C4

Head downstairs to this cosy restaurant, its walls lined with dusty bottles of wine. These are but a sample of more than 250 different varieties quietly maturing in El Tonique's cellars. The food is very good and worth the wait for a table (it's popular for lunch) and a plate of *setas con gambas* (oyster mushrooms with prawns). (📞922 26 15 29, www.tascaeltonique.es; Calle Heraclio Sánchez 23; mains €8.50-12; ⏱1-5pm & 8-11pm Tue-Sat, 8-11pm Mon)

Capricho Libanés
LEBANESE €

12 ✖️ Map p52, C2

This tiny place holds just a few tables, but they are normally full of happily chomping locals here for the tasty and authentic Lebanese food. Expect all the familiar dishes like hummus, felafel, tabbouleh and kebabs, while daily spe-

✅ Top Tip

Tipping
Menu prices include a service charge. Most people leave some small change if they're satisfied; 5% is normally fine and 10% extremely generous. Porters will generally be happy with €1. Taxi drivers don't have to be tipped but a little rounding up won't go amiss.

cials feature more unusual homestyle Middle Eastern dishes. There are also healthy soups, like carrot and pumpkin, and honey-soaked baklava for dessert. (📞922 25 29 93; Calle Núñez de la Peña 5; mains €9-10; ⏱11am-11pm Mon-Sat)

Drinking

Bar 7 Vies
BAR

13 🥤 Map p52, D3

Enjoy chill-out music and a cozy interior with burgundy walls and Victoriana decor. Although this is more a bar than restaurant, there are tapas and a reasonable daily *menú* on offer. Gets packed out with the local business bunch post clock-out time. (📞922 25 73 23; Calle Viana 35; ⏱8am-11.30pm; 🛜)

Casa Viña
BAR

14 🥤 Map p52, B2

One of the best pavement settings for sipping a drink and watching folk on the move. Close to the magnificent Iglesia de Nuestra Señora de la

Concepción, this *vinoteca* is owned by the well-respected Viña Norte winery based in Tacoronte. Enjoy a glass of their wine for just a couple of euros; good tapas also available. (☏922 63 37 29; www.bodegasinsulares.es; Plaza Concepción; ⏱11am-midnight Mon-Thu, to 3am Fri & Sat; ☏)

Coffee Break
CAFE

15 ⏱ Map p52, C2

Step into this urban-vibe cafe to be warmly embraced by a vivid wraparound frieze of La Laguna. Drinks and tasty bites, including waffles and cakes, add an extra sweet note. Plus there is live music on Saturdays, mainly in the soulful jazz genre. (☏822 66 24 84; Calle Capitán Brotons 2; ⏱7.30am-2pm & 5-9pm Mon-Fri, to midnight Sat; ☏)

La Pera Limonera
JUICE BAR

16 ⏱ Map p52, C2

A convivial and contemporary tight-squeeze space for enjoying healthy fruit and veg juices or coffee. Savoury snacks and a selection of delectable sweet-tooth delights also available. (☏922 26 71 59; Calle San Agustín 29; ⏱8.30am-7.30pm Mon-Fri, 9am-1.30pm Sat; ☏)

Bar Benidorm
BAR

17 ⏱ Map p52, A1

Don't let the name put you off; there's no HP Sauce on the tables here. This is a popular local bar which is known for its delicious *bocata de jamón* (ham sandwich), sliced fresh from one of the hams gently curing over the bar (thankfully not in cigarette smoke these days). The atmosphere is always bustling; note the extended opening hours! (☏922 25 88 62; Plaza Doctor Olivera 6; ⏱6am-midnight)

Pub Gabbana
CLUB

18 ⏱ Map p52, C5

A heaving nightclub that is also increasingly popular for its karaoke nights and contests – just in case you feel a Whitney Houston moment coming on. Located in the heart of the clubbing area and generally packed with a lively bunch of students. (☏922 00 00 00; Calle Doctor Antonio González 11; ⏱6pm-2am)

Shopping

Tea & Baking
FOOD

19 Map p52, C3

The name says it all. This colourful lip-smacking shop sells everything to do with baking, ranging from cooking chocolate to fancy bowls, printed aprons, rose water and, yes, even Reese's peanut-butter chips for poor deprived Americans. Also stocks some one-off items like Crabtree & Evelyn biscuits and the tantalisingly exotic pomegranate green tea from Arizona. (www.teaandbaking.es; Calle Capitán Brotóns 3; ⊘10am-1.30pm & 5-7pm Mon-Fri, to 1.30pm Sat)

El Rincon Extremeño
FOOD

20 Map p52, B2

A good place to buy *jamón ibérico de bellota* (ham from acorn-fed black pigs) priced at around €40 a kilo. Other less expensive hams are also available, either a whole leg or, if this equals a worrying protuberance from your hand luggage, sliced and shrink wrapped. You can also enjoy a taster (€1.80 to €4), also of cheese, including the prize-winning Majorero from Fuerteventura. (☑922 26 65 08; www.elrinconextremeno.net; Plaza Concepción 1; ⊘10am-2.30pm & 5.30-10.30pm Mon-Sat, 10am-2pm Sun)

Dicky Morgan
VINTAGE

21 Map p52, C2

Look for the blue-on-blue exterior of this fabulous vintage shop with its

Local Life

Linares

A wonderful old-fashioned haberdashery, **Linares** (Map p52, B3; Calle Herradores 69-71; ⊘9am-2pm & 5-7pm Mon-Fri, to 2pm Sat) has 'fashions' still firmly in the 1950s, like woolly men's cardigans with leather buttons and quilted dressing gowns in fetching floral fabrics. There are also great bolts of all kinds of materials and original wooden fittings, furniture and (quite possibly) sales staff.

edgy take on fashion, furniture and art, coupled with a big city outlook and a fun sense of humour. (☑922 26 70 04; www.dickymorganvintage.tumblr.com; Calle San Agustín 75; ⊘10.30am-1.30pm & 5-8pm)

Albacería
FOOD & DRINK

22 Map p52, C3

This old-fashioned grocery shop, bizarrely surrounded by smart boutiques and shops, dates from 1952 and may well bring on a dose of nostalgia as the interior seems little changed from yesteryear. It's a good place to pick up some fresh fruit and inexpensive deli items where you pay for the product rather than the packaging. (☑922 25 93 31; Calle Herradores 49; ⊘10am-2pm & 6-8.30pm Mon-Fri, 10am-2pm Sat)

Explore

Puerto de la Cruz

Puerto is a delight; a former spa destination for genteel Victorian ladies, the town still exudes plenty of character, with stylish boardwalks, a leafy central plaza, stunning gardens and a picturesque, albeit mildly rundown, harbour. This is also a serious foodie town, particularly in the former fishing district of La Ranilla, where some of the most innovative new bars and restaurants are located.

The Sights in a Day

☀ First up, head to the **Casa de la Aduana** (p74) to visit the **Museo de Arte Contemporáneo** (p68), duck into the gift shop here, and pick up a map at the tourist office. Enjoy a mid-morning coffee at **Ebano Café** (p73), then peek into the **Iglesia de Nuestra Señora de la Peña de Francia** (p69). Stroll to Plaza Charco checking out the shops en route.

☀ Have lunch at nearby **Regulo** (p72), then lace up your trainers and head to Puerto's magnificent gardens. Choose between the nearby **Sitio Litre Garden** (p68) or the **Jardín Botánico** (p62) (you'll need to hop in a taxi for the latter), before heading back to the centre. Stop at **Terraza Taoro** (p73) for a restorative cold drink and continue to **Risco Belle Aquatic Gardens** (p63).

☾ Duck into the **Museo Arqueológico** (p69) before it closes, then follow the music to Plaza Charco (traditional bands play here at dusk), and have a drink at centre-stage **Bar Dinámico** (p73). Explore La Ranilla's backstreets and opt for an innovative veggie dinner at **El Maná** (p71). Finish off your day toe-tapping to the live music at **Blanco Bar** (p74).

For a local's day in Puerto de la Cruz, see p64.

Top Experiences

Jardín Botánico (p62)

◎ Local Life

A Fishy Trail (p64)

♥ Best of Puerto de la Cruz

Eating

Selma & Louisa (p71)

La Rosa di Bari (p71)

Regulo (p72)

La Papaya (p72)

Shopping

La Ranilla (p74)

Licoreria Puerto (p75)

Lino Troska's (p75)

Casa de la Aduana (p74)

Parks & Gardens

Jardín Botánico (p62)

Sitio Litre Garden (p68)

Risco Belle Aquatic Gardens (p63)

Getting There

🚌 **Bus** There is a frequent TITSA bus service from Santa Cruz. Bus 103 (€5.25, 40 minutes) is direct while bus 102 travels via Tenerife Norte airport and La Laguna.

Top Experiences
Jardín Botánico

Puerto de la Cruz is home to several magnificent gardens and parks; the crowning glory is the Jardín Botánico, a lush subtropical garden that is primarily dedicated to the flora of the Canary Islands, with more than 30,000 specimens spread over some 2.5 hectares. It is a peaceful haven, with strategically located seating, plenty of bird-song, fragrant flowers and a meandering pathway that takes you on a fascinating botanical journey across the globe.

◉ Map p66, H4

☎ 922 92 29 81

Calle Retama 2

adult/child €3/free

⊘ 9am-6pm

Rubber tree in Jardín Botánico

Don't Miss

Discovering the History

Ask for the free brochure, which gives the fascinating background to the gardens. They were created by the Royal Order of Carlos III in 1788 as a staging post for cultivating plant and tree species imported from the tropics, with the eventual plan to introduce them to the royal gardens in Madrid. Unsurprisingly, the Spanish mainland proved too cool, so this second phase wilted away.

Extraordinary Trees

These gardens are a lost world of fairytale trees including the 200-year-old massive Australian Moreton bay fig, with its wall-like buttress roots; the reptilian monkey puzzle tree from the Andes; South American silk floss with bizarre spiky trunks of armour, and several varieties of palms, including the skyscraper *Phoenix carariensis*.

The Lily Pond

This is the perfect shady place to relax on a warm summer's day. And what better place to grab some bench time than overlooking a dreamy lily pond with sunbasking terrapins and darting dragonflies, against a subtropical backdrop of plants and trees. It's a world away from the clamour of the coast.

Nearby: Risco Belle Aquatic Gardens

Less than 1km west of Jardín Botánico, in Parque Taoro, the **Risco Belle Aquatic Gardens** (Map p66; Parque Taoro; adult/child €4/free; ⊙9.30am-6pm; P) resemble a Renoir canvas, the sweeping lawn frontage is studded with citrus trees, water features and tropical plants, as well as cafe tables and chairs. From here, hidden paths lead to a lily-filled lake with waterfalls and bridges where swooping herons and leisurely waterfowl add to the painterly setting.

☑ Top Tips

▶ Try and re-schedule your visit if you spy a tour bus outside; it can get crowded.

▶ Take water (and snacks for children); no refreshments are available on site.

▶ Pathways may be wet; wear sensible footwear.

▶ It's a long walk from the centre; several buses stop at the gardens en route out of town. Check www.titsa.com for a timetable.

✖ Take a Break

Opposite the entrance, the **Terraza del Botánico** (📞922 37 60 27; Calle Retama, edificio Retama 3; mains €10-15; ⊙noon-11pm) offers a relaxed setting for sampling innovative international cuisine. Alternatively, the splendid Hotel Botánico has several excellent restaurants, including **La Parrilla** (📞922 38 14 00; www.hotelbotanico.com; Avenida Richard J Yeoward 1; mains €10-16; ⊙noon-4pm & 6-11pm; P🛜), specialising in upmarket Spanish cuisine.

Local Life
A Fishy Trail

This charming multifaceted resort has its roots firmly in the seafaring and fishing industry. While the small harbour is physically and culturally still at the heart of the town, the surrounding tangled net of streets is one of the most fashionable parts of Puerto for locals-in-the-know, with its terraced bars and scenic squares.

① Harbour Bars

Join the local fisherfolk at **Bar La Muelle** (Calle Mequínez 1; ⏲6am-7pm Mon-Sat), a gritty local place on the harbour serving the best *carallijo* (coffee and brandy) in town. Note the opening time: if you get here early enough, you may just catch the fishing boats as they return to this tiny port with its unpretentious charm.

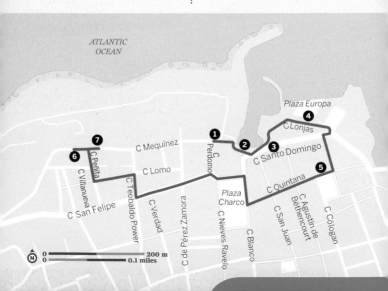

2 Jamónes Riviera

The market-style stall of **Jamónes Riviera** (Harbour; ⊙9am-10pm) is a daily institution, where the locals come to stock up on all those deli goodies, aside from seafood, including cheese, chorizo and the famous *jamón serrano* (Serrano ham), which can be sold vacuum-packed if you are looking for a particularly salivatory souvenir to impress the folks back home.

3 Calle Santo Domingo

This shopping street has a couple of gems on it, including **Rhodian House** (Calle Santo Domingo 4; ⊙10am-1.30pm & 4-8pm Mon-Fri, to 1.30pm Sat), selling jewellery made from natural abalone and seashells, and **Marysol** (Calle Santo Domingo 6; ⊙10am-8pm Mon-Sat), one of the first shops to open here back in the '80s, specialising in fine jewellery made with coral, lava and silver.

4 Fresh-off-the-Boat Seafood

Owned by the local fishermen, the **Confradía de Pescadores** (Calle Lonjas 5; mains €12-20, ⊙noon-3pm; **P**) is quite simply the best place for eating seafood and fish in town – unless you buy it fresh from the fish stall next door to cook yourself! Push the boat out with the lobster paella for two (€40).

5 Terraza Time

Located within confessional distance of the 17th-century *iglesia*, surrounded by a pretty park and fountain, **Terraza Marquesa** (⏲922 38 31 51; www.hotelmarquesa.com; Calle Quintana 11; ⊙8am-2am) fronts one of the town's oldest hotels and is a supreme spot for spying on strolling folk, and enjoying a long cold *cerveza* (beer). There's live Canarian music here nightly from 7.30pm – listen for that Latino beat.

6 La Ranilla

Continue to this pretty plaza in La Ranilla *barrio* where brightly coloured fishermen's cottages have been transformed into fashionable restaurants and bars, including **Agora** (Plazoleta de Benito Pérez Galdós 6, La Ranilla; ⊙10am-midnight; 🛜), a cafe and cocktail bar rolled into one with art exhibitions, books to borrow, magazines to read, games to play and impromptu salsa classes (even).

7 Calle Mequínez

Nip around the corner to this lively street, home to a handful of chilled-out places to eat and drink including **Bodega Julian** (⏲686 55 63 15; Calle Mequínez 20; mains €9-13; ⊙6pm-midnight Tue-Sun), with its reassuringly brief menu of specialities like cod on sweet potato and succulent roasted lamb. The owners are accomplished musicians so live music is an added plus.

A   B   C   D

ATLANTIC
OCEAN

Iglesia de Nuestra
Señora de la Peña
de Francia

Puerto
Pesquero

Museo de Arte   **28** Plaza
Contemporáneo **2**   Europa

31   **30**

22   **19** **14**   Iglesia
C Mequinez   **27**   C Peñita   **12**   de San   **32**
                 C Villanueva **13**   Museo   Francisco   **4**
                              15 **3** Arqueológico **5**
C San Felipe   **25**   C San Juan

                           C Verdad   **17**

C Puerto Viejo   **20**

C Dr Ingram   C Cupido

Castillo
de San
Felipe
8

Playa
Jardín   **10**
6   **El Cardumen**

11   Av Melchor Luz

Barranco San Felipe

Agustín de Béthencourt
C Cólogan
C Blanco   **16**
            26

C Nieves Ravelo

C le Sala   **21**
C Lomo Nieve

Carreterad

Parque
Taoro

E · F · G · H

N 0 ——————————— 500 m
0 ——————————— 0.25 miles

7 Lago Martiánez

9 Playa Martiánez

Av Colón

Av Venezuela

Paseo San Telmo

C Hoya

C Obispo

24

Betancourt y Molina

Pérez Cáceres

C Aguilar y Quesada

29

C Iriarte

Av Familia

C Zamora

C Dr Pisaca

C Esquivel

C Valois

Barranco Martiánez

Camino Robado

Camino San Amaro

Calzada Martiánez

Jardín Botánico

Risco Belle Aquatic Gardens

Taoro

Sitio Litre Garden **1**

Av Marquès Villanueva Prado

Experiences

Sitio Litre Garden

GARDENS

1 📍 Map p66, F4

This delightful garden is exquisitely laid out with walkways, fountains, tropical and subtropical plants and flowers, plus the oldest *drago* (dragon) tree in town. The highlight is the orchid walk-through greenhouse with its well-displayed and -signed orchids. There is an inviting terrace cafe and a (surprisingly tacky) gift shop. The gardens have an interesting British-based history, which you can read about in the free leaflet. (www.jardindeorquideas.com; Camino Robado; adult/child €4.75/free; ⏱9.30am-5pm)

Museo de Arte Contemporáneo

ART

2 📍 Map p66, D2

The first contemporary art museum to open in Spain, dating from 1953, this well-displayed collection includes such outstanding foreign, Spanish and Canarian artists as Will Faber, Óscar Domínguez and César Manrique. The setting, in the historic former customs house, is almost as inspiring as the art-

Understand

Cochineal

This natural red dye is produced by a beetle that lives on the prickly pear cactus which you see growing in the wild throughout Tenerife, including Puerto de la Cruz. The story goes that it was discovered by the Spanish in Mexico in the 16th century and brought to Europe, where they initially claimed it was produced by seeds (probably because that sounds marginally more appealing than ground-up beetles...especially for lipstick!).

Cochineal was a major export in Tenerife in the 1850s, with prickly pears replacing the vines which had become diseased by grape louse, thus destroying the formerly lucrative viticulture industry. The dye is produced by the female cochineal beetle who drives her tubular proboscis through the cactus skin, where she remains happily affixed for the rest of her life, sucking out the juice. At the same time, she produces a waxy, white coating which acts as a kind of armour from predatory birds and insects. After around three months, the beetles are removed from the cacti and left to dry, after which they are ground up to extract the dye. Approximately 70,000 cochineal insects are required to manufacture a single pound of crimson dye.

The introduction of synthetic dyes in the late 19th century led to the demise of the cochineal industry although cochineal is reputedly still used by the pharmaceutical industry to colour pills and ointments (look for the word carmine on the list of ingredients).

work. (Casa de la Aduana, Calle Lonjas; adult/child €1.50/free; ⊙10am-2pm Mon-Sat)

Museo Arqueológico   MUSEUM

3 ◉ Map p66, C3

This small but well laid-out museum provides an insight into the Guanche way of life with its replicas of a typical cave dwelling, as well as a burial cave with pots and baked-clay adornments, demonstrating the Guanches' belief in an afterlife. The most interesting exhibit is a tiny clay idol – one of only a few ever found. (Archaeological Museum; www.museosdetenerife.org; Calle Lomo 9; adult/child €1/free; ⊙10am-1pm & 5-9pm Tue-Sat, 10am-1pm Sun)

Iglesia de Nuestra Señora de la Peña de Francia   CHURCH

4 ◉ Map p66, D3

This pretty 17th-century church boasts three naves, a wooden Mudéjar ceiling and the image of Gran Poder de Dios, one of the town's most revered saints. The church is fronted by lush landscaped gardens. (Calle Quintana; ⊙8am-6pm)

Iglesia de San Francisco   CHURCH

5 ◉ Map p66, D3

Located just off Puerto's central (and famed) Plaza del Charco is the Iglesia de San Francisco, tacked on to tiny Ermita de San Juan, the oldest structure in town (built in 1599). (Calle Quintana; ⊙variable opening hours)

Iglesia de Nuestra Señora de la Peña de Francia

Playa Jardín   BEACH

6 ◉ Map p66, A4

This dark-sand 'garden beach' west of the centre has good facilities, including toilets and showers. Huge boulders and rocks were dumped in the sea here to prevent the sand being swept away. (Paseo Luis Lavagi; P)

Lago Martiánez   SWIMMING

7 ◉ Map p66, F2

Designed by Canario César Manrique, the watery playground of Lago Martiánez has four saltwater pools and a large central 'lake'. It can get just as crowded as the surrounding small volcanic beaches. Swim, sunbathe or grab a bite at one of the many restaurants and bars. (📞922 37 05 72; Avenida Colón; adult/child €3.50/1.20; 🕙10am-sunset)

Castillo de San Felipe

CASTLE

8 ◎ Map p66, A4

This modest castle located beside Playa Jardín, plays host to a variety of temporary art exhibitions and regular theatre and dance performances. It was closed for refurbishment at research time, however; check at the tourist office for an update. (📞922 37 30 39; Paseo Luis Lavaggi 12)

Q Local Life
Quirky Festivals

Aside from a riotous Carnaval celebration, Puerto has some other fun-filled, and thoroughly weird, fiestas:

San Juan Held on the eve of the saint's day (23 June). Bonfires light the sky and, in a throwback to Guanche times, goats are driven for a dip in the sea off Playa Jardín.

Fiesta de los Cacharros Takes place on 29 November, this is a quaint festival where children rush through the streets, dragging behind them a string of old pots, kettles, pans, car spares, tin cans – just about anything that will make a racket!

Playa Martiánez

BEACH

9 ◎ Map p66, G2

The long sandy Playa Martiánez is located at the eastern end of town. A large jetty filters down the anger of Atlantic swells and turns them into mere gentle rollers, perfect for learning to surf on. The beach itself consists of soft, black sand. (Avenida de Colón)

El Cardumen

DIVING, GLIDING

10 ◎ Map p66, B4

Offers a range of diving courses including an introductory 'try dive'. If you prefer to soar like a bird rather than swim like a fish, it also offers paragliding. (📞670 38 30 07; www.elcardumen.com; Avenida Melchor Luz 3)

Loro Parque

ZOO

11 ◎ Map p66, A4

Travelling around Tenerife, the Loro Parque flag is so ubiquitous that you could be forgiven for thinking they sponsor the island. But we'll give them their dues because where else can you see over 350 species of parrots (the world's largest collection) at once? Today its animal portfolio has grown to include tigers, gorillas and chimpanzees. Note that the park also keeps captive orcas and dolphins, which perform in popular shows; however, research indicates such captivity is debilitating and stressful for these creatures, and is exacerbated by human interaction. (📞922 37 38 41; www.loroparque.com; Avenida Loro Parque; adult/child €34/23; 🕙8.30am-6.45pm; 🅿)

Eating

El Maná   ORGANIC, VEGETARIAN €€

12 ✗ Map p66, C3

Choose from innovative, fresh and delicious dishes that obviously (being organic) change depending on what is fresh in the vegetable patch that week. Expect unusual combinations like handmade sour-apple ravioli with raisins, and vegetable couscous with an *ajoblanco* (almond-based) sauce. End on a sweet note with the vanilla-and-mango pannacotta. (www.elmana. es; Mequínez 21, La Ranilla; mains €9-16; ☺1-4pm & 7-10pm Wed-Sun; 🖋)

Selma & Louisa   SWEDISH €

13 ✗ Map p66, C3

Follow the enticing smell of freshly baked cinnamon rolls to this Swedish mother-and-daughter-run eco-friendly cafe, with its tasty breakfast choice including homemade granola, scrambled eggs and fluffy pancakes. The daily-made soups are equally good. Plus there are healthy sandwich combos, quiches and gorgeous cakes. (Calle Lomo 18, La Ranilla; breakfast €4.50-5; ☺8.30am-7pm Tue-Sun; 🖋)

Restaurante Mil Sabores   MEDITERRANEAN €€

14 ✗ Map p66, C2

Styling itself as a temple to modern Mediterranean cooking, this flash restaurant has the looks and the tastes down to a fine art. What sort of

Q Local Life
Guachinches

A garden shed, family sitting room, empty garage...these are just a few locations where you can find *guachinches*, no-frills eateries serving homecooked traditional meals for under a tenner. Particularly prevalent in the north, and very popular at weekends, *guachinches* are hard to find if you're not a local in the know. One way to savvy up is to download the Android or Apple app: guachapp. There is also a Guachinches de Tenerife Facebook page with regularly updated information, or ask at the tourist office.

things can you expect to find on the menu? How about a prawn lollipop with roasted corn and parmesan, or a perfectly combined mix of pork, apple and bacon? It's quite dressy without being formal. Reservations recommended. (📞922 36 81 72; Calle Cruz Verde 5, La Ranilla; mains €12-18; ☺noon-11pm)

La Rosa di Bari   ITALIAN €€

15 ✗ Map p66, C3

Located in a lovely old house with several romantic dining rooms, this unassuming little place is actually one of the classiest restaurants in town. Enjoy innovative dishes like black tagliatelle with courgettes and prawns, and fish with a mustard crust. (📞922 36 85 23; www.larosadibari.com; Calle Lomo 23, La Ranilla; mains €11-17; ☺12.30-2.45pm & 7-10.45pm Tue-Sat, 12.30-4pm Sun)

Local Life
Harbourside Churros

For the best churros in town, join the local fishermen at harbour-front **Churreria Perdomo** (Harbour; churros €1; ☉6am-6pm Mon-Sat) for a portion of these hot crispy spiral-shaped doughnuts dunked into hot chocolate. They also sell *porras* which are larger tubular doughnuts, also quick fried and utterly irresistible.

Tasca el Olivo   MEDITERRANEAN €€

16 ✕ Map p66, D3

The Mediterranean cuisine here is soundly prepared and spiked with just a soupçon of innovation. Surf-and-turf choices like pork loins with prawns win over the locals who rate this restaurant as one of the best in town. On the downside, the interior could up the intimacy stakes by losing a few light bulbs. (☎922 38 01 17; Calle Iriarte 1; mains €9-15; ☉1-4pm & 5-10.30pm Tue-Sun)

Regulo   CANARIAN €€

17 ✕ Map p66, C3

The setting is fairytale atmospheric; a 200-year-old building with creaky uneven floors, rustic antiques and small dining rooms covering three floors and set around a leafy central courtyard. The Canarian cuisine attracts a reassuring mix of locals and tourists with sophisticated, yet simple dishes like salmon in champagne. Service can be slow. (☎922 38 45 06; www.restauranteregulo.com; Calle de Pérez Zamora 16; mains €9-15; ☉6pm-1am Mon, 12.30-3pm & 6-11pm Tue-Sat)

El Limón   VEGETARIAN €

18 ✕ Map p66, D3

A bright vegetarian restaurant with a menu consisting of veggie burgers, seitan kebabs, salads and fresh fruit juices, among others. It also does a good-value set-lunch menu (€10) and the clientele is almost exclusively local. (Calle Esquivel 4; mains €7-10; ☉noon-11pm Mon-Sun; 🖋)

La Papaya   CANARIAN €€

19 ✕ Map p66, C3

This long-time favourite has a series of small dining rooms with rock-face walls and a pretty patio set around a magnificent tree draped with bougainvillea. There are Canarian touches to the menu, including the succulent salmon in *malvasía* (Malmsey wine) sauce, plus a wide choice for children. (☎922 38 28 11; Calle Lomo 10, La Ranilla; mains €10-16; ☉noon-4pm & 7-11pm Thu-Tue; 👶)

Meson los Gemelos   CANARIAN €

20 ✕ Map p66, C3

This is a friendly, welcoming restaurant with a great atmosphere; the house speciality is grilled meats. There's a covered interior barn-size patio decorated with hanging plants, leafy ferns and agricultural paraphernalia. Increasingly popular with tourists, you can expect queues at the door. Reserve ahead if possible.

(📞922 37 01 33; Calle Peñón 4; mains €8-10; 🕙noon-11pm Thu-Tue; 🅿🚺)

Drinking

Terraza Taoro   BAR

21 🚇 Map p66, D4

Once you have clambored up the some 200 steps from the centre of town, you deserve a long cool drink; the panoramic views of the town and coast from the sweeping terrace here are a bonus. Speciality coffees and fancy cocktails are justifiably popular; sweet and savoury snacks also available. (📞922 38 88 68; www.terrazataoro.com; Carretera de Taoro 9; 🕙10am-10pm)

La Tasquita Flamenca   BAR

22 🚇 Map p66, B3

Get duly frilled and polka dotted and head to this tiny Andalusian bar with live flamenco guitar music nightly and a menu of traditional southern Spain tapas, including grilled prawns (from Huelva) and crisp-fried aubergines drizzled with sugar-cane molasses, a Málaga specialty. (Calle Mequínez 49; 🕙1pm-midnight Tue-Sun)

Ebano Café   CAFE

23 🚇 Map p66, D3

This is a beautiful building with plenty of original features and which is equally ideal for sipping a cocktail or surfing the web (along with a decent cappuccino). Sit outside in a comfy wicker chair within confessional distance of the church. Tapas also served. (Calle Hoya 2; 🕙10am-midnight; 🛜)

Azucar   CLUB

24 🚇 Map p66, F3

This dark and sexy Latino nightclub is located in an atmospheric colonial building. (Calle Obispo Pérez Cáceres; 🕙10.30pm-6am)

Colours Café   BAR

25 🚇 Map p66, C3

Above a pizzeria on an energetic stretch of eateries, this cocktail bar is the perfect spot to snag a window seat overlooking the square. With mellow decor and Latin and African music, it's a good place to kick off your night on the tiles. (Plaza Charco; 🕙8pm-2am Wed-Mon)

🔍 Local Life
Bar Dinámico

Bars and cafes come and go in Puerto but **Bar Dinámico** (www.dinamicopuertodelacruz.com; Plaza Charco; 🕙9am-midnight; 🛜) has been around since the '50s in one form or another, and has counted the Beatles and Agatha Christie among its patrons. It's a sprawling terraced place in the centre of Plaza Charco with a Latin American vibe and more local character than most places encircling the square.

Entertainment

Blanco Bar
LIVE MUSIC

26 ⭐ Map p66, D3

Check the website beforehand as, as well as live music, there are comedy acts, which may not affect your tickle bone unless you speak Spanish. Also hosts art exhibitions and has a great atmosphere with no rip-off drinks prices plus free entry to the concerts. (📞620 95 51 97; www.blancobar.com; Calle Blanco 12; ⊘8pm-3am Sun-Thu, 9pm-5.30am Fri & Sat; 🛜)

Shopping

La Ranilla
HANDICRAFTS

27 🔒 Map p66, B3

Look for a tiny former fisherman's cottage painted brilliant turquoise and now the happy home to this crafts shop specialising in innovative local handmade art and handcrafts including jewellery, ceramics, textiles and toys. No straw donkeys here. Instead, look for vividly coloured earrings made from CDs or handmade marionettes. (📞922 38 50 87; www.laranillaespacioartesano.com; Calle Mequínez 59; ⊘10am-2pm & 5-7pm Mon-Sat)

Casa de la Aduana
CRAFTS

28 🔒 Map p66, D2

The most comprehensive selection of quality crafts in town. A little pricey but this is no souvenir tat. The range includes classy locally produced jewellery, finely crafted ceramics, stone and glassware, quirky children's toys, elegant hand-painted fans and tasteful textiles (with not an *I Love Tenerife* T-shirt in sight). The adjacent delicatessen and

---

Understand
Tenerife Tipple

The wine of Tenerife (and the Canaries in general) isn't well known internationally, but it is starting to earn more of a name for itself. The best-known, and first to earn the DO grade (*Denominación de Origen*), which certifies high standards and regional origin, is the red Tacoronte Acentejo. Also worth a tipple are the wines produced in Icod de los Vinos and Güímar. The **Casa del Vino La Baranda** (📞922 57 25 35; www.casadelvinotenerife.com; Autopista del Norte, El Sauzal; admission free; ⊘10.30am-6.30pm Tue, 9am-9pm Wed-Sat, 11am-6pm Sun; 🅿) in nearby El Sauzal organises regular wine-appreciation courses. This museum is well worth a visit. Located in a traditional Canarian country house, the museum is devoted to wine and its production and there is an opportunity to sample local wines for a nominal cost. Other local tipples include La Dorada beer, brewed in Santa Cruz de Tenerife, its lager-style taste equal to any import from the mainland.

bodega specialises in local wines and gourmet products. (☑922 37 81 03; Calle Lonjas 8-10; ⊙10am-8pm Mon-Sat)

Licoreria Puerto
FOOD & DRINK

29 🅰 Map p66, E3

The place to stock up on a few edible mementos from a wide array of Canarian specialties including banana wine (available for tasting), *mojo* spices, aloe vera products and ecological preserves, honey, spreads, cactus marmalade and sweets. (☑922 38 18 15; Calle Hoya 22; ⊙10am-1.30pm & 5-7.30pm Mon-Fri, to 2pm Sat)

Lino Troska's
ACCESSORIES

30 🅰 Map p66, D2

Sells a limited but tasteful array of exquisitely painted silk garments and scarves plus their speciality – ceramics, decorative items and jewellery created from volcanic lava combined with silver, gold, semi-precious stones or minerals – all made by Canarian-based artisans and designers. (☑619 53 11 60; Calle Santo Domingo 7; ⊙10am-8pm Mon-Sat)

Carey
FASHION

31 🅰 Map p66, C2

An enchanting small boutique selling beautifully crafted jewellery, designer-look women's fashion and casual chic accessories, including sequined belts and glittery evening bags. (☑922 38 87 23; Calle Mequínez 13; ⊙10am-2pm & 5-7.30pm Mon-Fri, to 2pm Sat)

Understand
Live Music

Puerto de la Cruz has one of the best live-music scenes in Tenerife. Most restaurants and many bars have regular musicians and, contrary to what you may think, this is not naff Benidorm-style entertainment; on the contrary, competition is rife and the standard surprisingly high. The music you hear will generally have a sizzling Latin beat, due to the considerable South American influence. Head for Plaza Charco around dusk where local bands regularly busk; there's plenty of space for dancing too – after a mojito or two, you may well be tempted...

Atlantico Shop
CLOTHING

32 🅰 Map p66, D2

The leather goods sold here are sourced in Morocco but, no, the souk tradition of haggling doesn't apply here. The quality-to-price ratio is good however, and the range is extensive and includes shoes, belts, coats and bags displayed in a vast showroom. On the downside, some of the designs look somewhat dated and some punchier colours would be good to see. (☑922 37 51 24; Calle Santo Domingo 12; ⊙9.30am-2pm & 5-8pm Mon-Sat)

Explore

La Orotava

This colonial town has the lot it seems: cobblestone streets, flower-filled plazas and more Castilian mansions than the rest of the island put together. La Orotava is one of the loveliest towns on Tenerife, surrounded by lush valleys which are home to bananas, chestnuts and vineyards, as well as being criss-crossed by picturesque foot-paths for anyone keen on striding out.

The Sights in a Day

☀ Start your visit at the fascinating **Museo de las Alfombras** (p85). Next, duck into the **Casa del Turista** (p85) for a spot of souvenir shopping, then cross the road to admire the **Casa de los Balcones** (p78) showrooms of crafts. Pop in for a coffee in the wonderful courtyard setting of **Tascafe Grimaldi** (p88), before admiring the baroque extravagance of the **Iglesia de la Concepción** (p86).

☀ After a belt-loosening meal at **Bar la Duquesa** (p87), enjoy a bench snooze in the fragrant **Hijuela del Botánico** (p86) garden. Head down the road to explore the cascading terraced gardens of the **Jardínes del Marquesado de la Quinta Roja** (p83). Next it's time to seek out that well-earned *cerveza* (beer) at **Tapias La Bodega** (p86).

☽ Stroll a couple of doors down to the tourist office to check out special events that night. Browse the shops on this street and pick up some *jamón* (and cheese) at **Depatanegra Ibericos** (p89). Stride out to the **Museo de Artesania Iberoamericana** (p83), then double back to the town's most happening nightlife square and a drink at **La Tasca de Bullicio** (p88). Stay on for dinner or shimmy next door to upbeat **El Aliño** (p88).

For a local's day in La Orotava, see p80.

Top Experience

Casa de los Balcones (p78)

🔍 Local Life

Timeless Tascas & Crafts (p80)

♥ Best of La Orotava

Traditional Cuisine

La Tesela (p81)

Sabor Canario (p86)

Tapias La Bodega (p86)

Tascafe Grimaldi (p88)

Historical Architecture

Casa de los Balcones (p78)

Casa del Turista (p85)

Museo de Artesania Iberoamericana (p83)

Casa Torrehermosa (p81)

Liceo de Taoro (p81)

Getting There

🚌 **Bus** From nearby Puerto de la Cruz, TITSA bus 345 (€1.45, 20 minutes) leaves roughly every half-hour from 5.40am to 9.55pm.

🚕 **Taxi** A taxi from Puerto de la Cruz will cost around €10.

Top Experiences
Casa de los Balcones

La Orotava has been able to preserve the beauty of the past. Traditional mansions are flanked with ornate wooden balconies like pirate galleons, revealing sumptuous inner courtyards and surrounded by manicured gardens. Calle San Francisco is home to the highest concentration of 17th-century architectural gems, dating from the time when the town was home to Tenerife's wealthiest aristocrats. Arguably the most representative of the traditional balconied mansions here is the justifiably popular Casa de los Balcones.

Map p82, A4

www.casa-balcones.com

Casa Fonseca, Calle San Francisco 3

admission free

8.30am-6.30pm

Don't Miss

Culture & Crafts

Ground-floor rooms are set around a leafy central patio packed with memorabilia. One room is devoted to lacework, where you can admire the fine local needlework; there may be a demonstration too. There's also a traditional *bodega* where you can ask for a taste of the banana liquor.

Museum

Many tourists don't stray further than the ground-floor exhibition and sales space, missing out on the delightfully quirky 1st-floor museum. Rooms are furnished with 17th-century antiques; the granny in bed will make you smile. This is also the best place for photographing the building, with fabulous views of the courtyard below with its intricate woodwork carving.

Nearby: Casa Lercaro

This 16th-century **mansion** (www.casalercaro.com; Calle Colegio 5-7; ⏱restaurant 10am-7pm Sun-Wed, to 11pm Thu & Fri) is widely considered to be the most representative building constructed in traditional Canary Island style. Particularly noteworthy is the finely carved baroque decoration on the woodwork, including the magnificent traditional balconies. The interior plant-filled courtyard is now a restaurant; look for the 17th-century sculpture entitled *Adoración de los Pastores* from the Genoa school. Part of the building also houses a decor shop.

VII OF 101/SHUTTERSTOCK ©

☑ Top Tips

▶ This sight is very popular with tour groups, so try and visit early in the morning or in the late afternoon, if possible.

▶ Parking nearby is difficult and restricted, so come by bus or taxi if you can.

▶ Drop by the tourist office to pick up a map of other grand historic mansions around La Orotava, many of which are near Casa de los Balcones.

✗ Take a Break

Grab a chair on the terrace and enjoy a mid-morning tapa at the reliable local Bar la Duquesa (p87). Or swoon at the valley views from Tascafe Grimaldi (p88) along with a drink or something more filling.

Local Life
Timeless Tascas & Crafts

Tucked in between leafy court-yards and steep winding streets are shops selling beautifully made local crafts and gourmet items, while cultural history is kept alive via still-functioning mills. And if you hear that distinctive slap of dominoes, follow the sound, as it will doubtless take you to one of the town's numerous old-fashioned bars *(tascas)*; great for inexpensive tapas – and atmosphere.

❶ Café los Balcones
Bypassed by tourists marching past to the centre of town, the **Café los Balcones** (Calle San Francisco 10; breakfast €3-5; ⊙8am-7pm) is a no-frills cafe-cum-*tasca* set in a historic building and a great place to kickstart your day with excellent coffee along with a *tostada con tomate* (toast topped with tomatoes and olive oil). Omelettes and such also available.

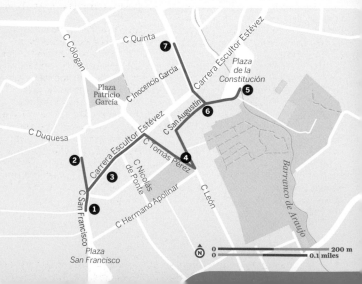

❷ La Maquina, Molino de Gofio

Once the staple diet of the Guanches, *gofio* is basically milled wheat and corn with the consistency of whole-grain flour. At **La Maquina** (📞922 33 07 03; Calle San Francisco ; 🕐8am-1pm & 2.30-6.30pm Mon-Fri, 9.30am-1pm Sat) you can watch the miller at work grinding the grain and buy a small bag of *gofio* (€1.50; raw or combined with cinnamon, chocolate or vanilla). Use it sprinkled on cereal or desserts.

❸ Canarian Handicrafts

As the name implies, **Canarias Concept** (www.canariasconcept.com; Calle Carrera Escultor 23; 🕐10am-7pm Mon-Sat) sells solely Canarian-made crafts and products with a large showroom packed with jewellery, ceramics, artwork, handmade toys and ornaments, plus a gourmet section with goodies like palm honey, cactus-based spreads, *tortas de almendras* (almond biscuits) and local wines.

❹ Torta Time

Founded in 1916, **Casa Egon** (Calle León 5; cakes €0.80-1; 🕐10am-8.30pm) is the oldest cake shop in the Canaries and has happily maintained its stuck-in-a-time-warp ambience with custard-coloured paintwork, antique weighing scales, and original floor tiles and much of the decor. The cakes include all-time local favourites *anís*-based *roscos* and *cabello de angel* (apple-filled cakes).

❺ Liceo de Taoro

The 19th-century **Liceo de Taoro** (www.liceodetaoro.es; 🕐9am-11pm Mon-Sun) has a magnificent setting high above the square. Now a private club, you can still order a drink from the bar within, and take it to the front terrace overlooking the ornamental gardens planted with birds of paradise and poinsettias, to the rooftops beyond.

❻ La Tesela

Join the flat-capped locals propping up the bar at **La Tesela** (Calle San Agustín 9; tapas €2, mains €7-9; 🕐11am-1pm & 4-8pm Wed-Sun), an earthy *tasca* fronting an animated pensioners' club with tapas like homemade croquettes and tortilla, along with heartier mains like goat stew. Drinks include the surprise of milkshakes, as well as local wines.

❼ Casa Torrehermosa

Tenerife's excellent art-and-crafts chain, Artenerife has its local outlet in this magnificent 17th-century mansion. **Casa Torrehermosa** (www.artenerife.com; Calle Tomás Zerolo 27; 🕐10am-5pm Mon-Fri, to 1pm Sat) provides a fitting setting for the display of locally produced artwork, pottery, jewellery and crafts, ranging from delicate hand-painted fans to original ceramics and glassware. You can also pick up local gourmet treats, as well as *gofio* from the original La Orotava mill.

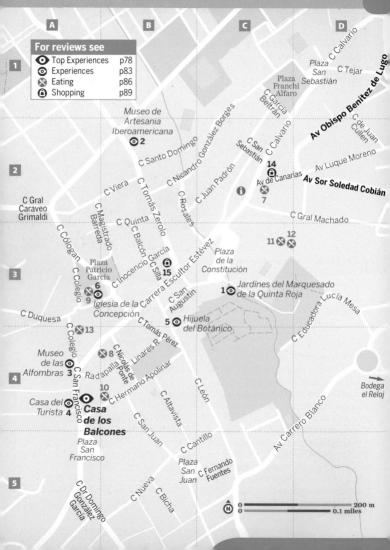

For reviews see
- Top Experiences　p78
- Experiences　p83
- Eating　p86
- Shopping　p89

Museo de Artesanía Iberoamericana ⊙2

Plaza San Sebastián

Plaza Franchi Alfaro

C Calvario
C Tejar

Av Obispo Benítez de Lugo

C de Juan Cullen

C García Beltrán

C San Sebastián
C Calvario

C Santo Domingo

Av Luque Moreno

C Nicandro González Borges

14 🔒
Av de Canarias
Av Sor Soledad Cobián

ℹ 7

C Viera

C Juan Padrón

C Tomás Zerolo

C Quinta

C Magistrado Barreda

C Rosales

C Gral Machado

C Balcón

C Gral Caraveo Grimaldi

11 ❌ 12 ❌

C Cólogan

Plaza Patricio García

C Inocencio García

C Silla

Plaza de la Constitución

6 ⊙
9 ❌

🔒 15

Iglesia de la Concepción

C Carrera Escultor Estévez

C San Agustín

1 ⊙ Jardínes del Marquesado de la Quinta Roja

C Colegio

C Duquesa

C Colegio

❌13

C Tomás Pérez

5 ⊙ Hijuela del Botánico

C Educadora Lucía Mesa

Museo de las Alfombras

❌ 3

❌8

C Nicolás de Ponte

C Radapalla
Linares R

C San Francisco

10 ❌

C Hermano Apolinar

C Altavista

C León

Bodega el Reloj

Casa del Turista 4

Casa de los Balcones

C San Juan

C Cantillo

Av Carrero Blanco

Plaza San Francisco

Plaza San Juan

C Fernando Fuentes

C Dr Domingo González García

C Nueva

C Bicha

0　　　200 m
0　　　0.1 miles

Jardínes del Marquesado de la Quinta Roja

Experiences

Jardínes del Marquesado de la Quinta Roja
GARDENS

1 📍 Map p82, C3

Also known as the Jardín Victoria, these French-influenced 18th-century gardens cascade down the hillside and are crowned by a small marble mausoleum built as a tomb for the Marqués de la Quinta Roja. However, apparently his wife and mother disagreed where to lay his body when he died, so the crypt was not used for its original purpose and no one knows what (or who) lies within. (Plaza de la Constitución; admission free; ⏰9am-6pm Mon-Fri, 10am-3pm Sat & Sun)

Museo de Artesania Iberoamericana
MUSEUM

2 📍 Map p82, B2

Housed in the former Convento de Santo Domingo, this museum explores

✅ Top Tip

Arriving by Bus

If you are arriving by bus, tell the driver you would like to be dropped off in *el centro histórico* (historic centre) rather than at the bus station, the final stop and a 15-minute uphill walk away.

Understand
Volcanic Landscapes & Wildlife

The seven islands and six islets that make up the Canary Islands are little more that the tallest tips of a vast volcanic mountain range that lies below the Atlantic Ocean. Just babies in geological terms, the islands were thrown up 30 million years ago when tectonic plates collided, crumpling the land into mammoth mountains. After the initial creation, a series of volcanic eruptions put the final touches on the islands' forms.

El Teide
Tenerife is home to El Teide, the third largest volcano in the world. Teide is what is known as a shield volcano; it's huge and rises in a broad, gently angled cone to a summit that holds a steep-walled, flat-based crater. Although seemingly quiet, El Teide is by no means finished, although its last eruptive burp was a fairly innocuous affair which took place in 1909. The most you will probably see during your visit, however, are the albeit alarming wisps of hot air that can sometimes be spied around the peak.

Dragon Trees
Among the more curious trees you will see here is the giant posy-like *drago* (dragon tree), which can reach 18m in height and live for centuries. Icod de los Vinos, a small town in the northwest, is home to what is reputed to be the oldest *drago* tree in the world, at 1000 years. Now that's a lot of birthday candles...

Wildlife
There is wildlife out there, but it tends to be small and shy and largely undetected by the untrained eye. Lizards and birds are the biggest things you'll see, with about 200 species of birds — including five endemics, like the pretty blue chaffinch. And yes, before you ask, this is where canaries come from, but the wild cousins are of a much duller colour tan than the cage birds. If it's big animals you want, you need to turn to the ocean. The stretch of water between Tenerife and La Gomera is a traditional feeding ground for as many as 26 species of whales, and others pass through during migration, the most common being pilot whales, sperm whales and bottle-nose dolphins.

Casa del Turista

the cultural relationship between the Canaries and the Americas. Exhibits include musical instruments, ceramics and various artefacts. There is also an excellent gift shop. (Iberoamerican Handicrafts Museum; Calle Tomás Zerolo 34; adult/child €2/free; ⊙9am-6pm Mon-Fri, 9.30am 2pm Sat)

Museo de las Alfombras

MUSEUM

3 ⊙ Map p82, A4

This museum celebrates the town's Corpus Christi festival with its tradition of carpets created from flowers and coloured sands from El Teide. Set in a beautiful galleried mansion dating from 1642, the exhibits explain the history of the tradition, as well as the process. There is also a wonderfully atmospheric and grainy 10-minute black-and-white audiovisual presentation of past festivities. (Calle San Francisco 5; adult/child €2/free; ⊙10am-2pm Mon-Fri)

Casa del Turista

HISTORIC BUILDING

4 ⊙ Map p82, A4

The building was a former 16th-century convent and today houses an art-and-crafts shop that includes a permanent exhibit of a volcanic-sand carpet that is typical of those produced for the Corpus Christi celebrations. (Calle San Francisco 4; ⊙9am-6.30pm)

REDA &CO SRL/ALAMY ©

Hijuela del Botánico
GARDENS

5 Map p82, B3

This small, sweet botanical garden centred around a magnificent *drago* tree was created as a branch of the larger Jardín Botánico in Puerto de la Cruz. It is home to around 3000 plant varieties, as well as plenty of birds, butterflies and strategically located benches. (Calle León; admission free; ⏱10am-3pm Mon-Fri)

Iglesia de la Concepción
CHURCH

6 Map p82, A3

Right in the centre of town, the origins of this magnificent church date from 1516, however it was destroyed by the earthquakes of 1704 and 1705 and rebuilt in 1768. Today it is recognised as being one of the finest examples of baroque architecture in the entire archipelago, with its three-fronted facade and three 24-metre-high bell towers. (www.concepcionorotava. info; Plaza Patricia García; ⏱9am-8pm)

Eating

Tapias La Bodega
SPANISH $

7 Map p82, C2

Squeeze in with the locals at lunchtime and enjoy some hearty tapas at this atmospheric wood-panelled bar with its barrel tables and large chalkboard menu over the bar. Especially good for Basque-style *pintxos* (small pieces of bread topped with towering creations pinned in place with a toothpick), *bocadillos* (sandwich rolls) made with various seeded breads and fresh salads. (📞922 33 53 95; Avenida de Canarias 6; salads €6.50, pintxos €2.50; ⏱7.30am-11.30pm Mon-Sat)

Sabor Canario
CANARIAN $$

8 Map p82, B4

Exercise the taste buds with soul-satisfying traditional cuisine at this fabulous restaurant located in the leafy patio of the Hotel Rural Orotava.

Understand
Corpus Christi

Try to coincide your visit with the local holiday of Corpus Christi, which is celebrated with extravagance in La Orotava (the date changes annually, but it always takes place in June), with the laying of an intricately designed floral carpet on the streets, made from petals, leaves and branches. In Plaza del Ayuntamiento, a dazzling tapestry of biblical scenes is created using coloured sands from El Teide. If you do not manage to time your visit with the holiday, be sure to visit the Casa del Turista (p85), which has a carpet on permanent display, as well as the Museo de las Alfombras (p85), with its exhibition on the background of the tradition as well as the painstaking process, together with explanations and photographs.

Flower carpet celebrating Corpus Christi

The building itself is a wonderful old Canarian townhouse stuffed full of memorabilia. (www.hotelruralorotava.es; Hotel Rural Orotava, Carrera Escultor 17; mains €10-15; ⊙noon-3.30pm & 6-10pm Tue-Sat)

Bar la Duquesa
CANARIAN $

9 Map p82, A3

A family-run bar, the interior is a pleasing clutter of old photos, Virgin posters, decorative gourds and farming utensils. The menu includes sound local choices like lentil soup, paella and grilled pork, plus there are outside tables on the cobbles in the shadow of the church. (Plaza Patricio García 6; mains €7.50-10; ⊙7am-4pm Mon-Fri, 8am-3pm Sat; 👬)

Local Life
Aguamansa

Located between La Orotava and El Teide is the delightful small village of Aguamansa. Just beyond here, the road passes a number of parking areas away from which radiate an array of marked walking trails, which are very popular with locals at weekends and mapped out on large signs. The walking here is easy with only gentle inclines and short distances to cover, so perfect for gentle family strolling. Most of the routes twist in and out of a beautiful laurel forest.

Top Tip

Menú del Día

If you want to euro-economise one great way is to order the *menú del día* which many restaurants offer at lunchtime during the week, which generally costs from between €7 to €9. You will usually have a generous choice of around five or six starters, the same number of mains and (on the downside) just a couple of desserts; choose one of each course.

Restaurante Victoria

INTERNATIONAL $$

10 Map p82, B4

Dine in Hotel Rural Victoria's elegant atrium at this superb restaurant. Okay, so perhaps sticky toffee pudding is not the height of culinary sophistication but the Scottish chef stops short of serving mushy peas; and on the contrary, the presentation and flair in such dishes as duck confit with saffron and the Canarian classic, rabbit in *salmorejo* (a marinade of bay leaves, garlic and wine) with *mojo* potatoes are exemplary. (922 33 16 83; www.hotelruralvictoria.com; Calle Hermano Apolinar 8; mains €12-18; 1-3.30pm & 7.30-9.30pm;)

La Tasca de Bullicio

CONTEMPORARY CANARIAN $$

11 Map p82, C3

Hard to find (on the top of a carpark, no less!), but persevere, as this *tasca* (tapas bar) is fast becoming one of the most fashionable places in town. The menu is short and sharp with steaks, salads and seafood, and live music, generally jazz, pulls in the punters every Sunday at 5.30pm. There's an excellent wine list, as well. (676 39 90 89; Plaza Quinto Centenario; mains €9-12; 1pm-midnight Tue-Sun;)

El Aliño

FUSION $$

12 Map p82, C3

Chocolate-brown walls, edgy modern prints, bowls of red apples and pomegranate sangria – yes, this place has style. The menu is contemporary and varied with east to west dishes ranging from tempura and sushi to creamy risottos, savoury crêpes and carpaccio. (922 32 18 80; Plaza Quinto Centenario; mains €12-18; 1-4pm & 9-11pm Mon-Sat;)

Tascafe Grimaldi

CANARIAN $$

13 Map p82, A4

The main terrace of this historic 1624 mansion, with its sea views and *drago* tree, is the place to head on a balmy summer's evening. A laid-back cafe, lively bar and elegant restaurant rolled into one, the dishes here are based on meat and fish with fabulous steaks and some lighter fare, like pumpkin soup and homemade croquettes. (Casa Lercaro; 615 26 65 26; Calle Colegio 7; mains €10-15; 10.30am-7pm Sun-Wed, to 11pm Thu & Fri)

Shopping

MAIT
HANDICRAFTS

Housed in the former 17th-century convent of San Benito Abad (see 2 ⊙ Map p82, B2), this museum shop sells a fabulous range of Ibero-American art and crafts with an emphasis on central and south America. Brightly painted ornaments from Mexico, Peruvian knitwear, Argentinian woven rugs, toys, jewellery and textiles are all displayed in a dazzle of vivid colour in this spacious showroom. (Museo de Artesania Iberoamericana; ☎922 32 81 60; www.artenerife.com; Calle Tomás Zerolo 34; ☺9am-6pm Mon-Fri, 9.30am-2pm Sat)

Depatanegra Ibericos
FOOD & DRINK

14 🔒 Map p82, C2

Carries a superb range of Spanish hams including the highly desired *jamón iberico de bellota*, made from acorn-fed black pigs. Expect to pay around €15 per 100g. Hams are sold sliced up and vacuum-packed for easy packing. Other deli items include a wide choice of chorizo. Also sells local wines, palm honey and Canarian and Spanish cheese. (☎922 32 54 83; Avenida de Canarias 7; ☺10am-2pm & 5-8pm Mon-Fri, to 2pm Sat)

Understand

Lucha Canaria

Lucha canaria (Canarian wrestling) dates from the times of the Guanches and still takes place throughout the island; ask at any tourist office for information about fixtures. Most towns still have an arena large enough for the sport, which comprises twelve contestants in two teams pitted against each other in suitably bloodthirsty style (not one for the kids!).

Solera
FASHION

15 🔒 Map p82, D3

This boutique oozes originality and good taste, with women's garments in vibrant colours and designs and beautiful silky fabrics. Also sells a small selection of soft leather bags in pretty pastel colours with a variety of designs, ranging from evening clutches to carry-your-entire-personal-life-along size satchels. (☎922 33 03 24; Calle Tomás Zerola 6; ☺10am-2pm Mon-Fri, to 2pm Sat)

Explore

Los Cristianos

Full of contradictions, Los Cristianos has, on the one hand, a kiss-me-quick reputation of karaoke bars and all-day English breakfasts. On the other, it is known for its superb city beach and watersports, its quirky independent shops, its great seafood and a small traditional centre, which still reflects a semblance of Canarian character with old-time bars (frequented by old-time locals).

CHRIS HEPBURN/GETTY IMAGES ©

The Sights in a Day

☼ Walk past the marching rows of concrete tower blocks that lead from the motorway to the coast, stopping en route for a healthy breakfast at **Sopa** (p98). Duck into the **Centro Cultural** (p97) to check out any exhibitions, then continue via the historic centre and **Librería Barbara** (p100), an old-fashioned international bookshop, to pick up a blockbuster for sunbed time.

☀ Grab a bite to eat at one of the food stands at **La Pepa Food Market** (p98), then carry on to the promenade, heading towards the harbour kiosks, where you can choose among a number of watersports and boat trips, including an introductory dive with **Club de Buceo** (p97). Pick up an ice-cream cone at **Riva Dulce** (p99) and kick back on the beach.

☾ Slip into sophisticated mode and sip a cocktail at the **Beach House** (p100). Have a stroll around the shops, then join the locals for a tapa at cloth-cap authentic **Tasca Nano** (p98). Head back to the promenade where the action is picking up and enjoy a stroll along the seafront, before sitting down to a slap-up seafood dinner at **Rincón del Marinero** (p97).

For a local's day in Los Cristianos, see p94.

Top Experiences

Watersports (p92)

○ Local Life

Backstreet Los Cristianos (p94)

♥ Best of Los Cristianos

Local Cuisine

Tasca Nano (p98)

Restaurante Fortuna Nova (p98)

El Cine (p97)

Diving

Club de Buceo (p97)

Shopping

Tina (p95)

Olé Espacio Gourmet (p101)

La Alpizpa (p100)

Librería Barbara (p100)

Getting There

🚌 **Bus** Plenty of TITSA buses come through the area, stopping at Los Cristianos. Buses 110 (direct, €9.70, one hour, every 30 minutes) and 111 (indirect) come and go from Santa Cruz. Bus 343 (€3.70, 45 minutes) goes to Tenerife Sur airport. Check www.titsa.com for a full schedule.

Top Experiences
Watersports

Playa de Los Cristianos' grand swathe of pale
golden sand is flanked to the east by a harbour
that is home to fishing boats, private yachts and
commercial boats offering everything from boat
rides to big game-fishing trips. Waters here drop
to dramatic depths and the combination of caves,
a temperate climate and the diverse ocean life
create ideal conditions for diving. Wind- and kite-
surfing are also popular, together with the most
obvious – a gentle paddle in the sea.

👁 Map p96, B4

Puerto de Los Cristianos,
Los Cristianos

Playa de Los Cristianos

Don't Miss

Try Dive

Consider Los Cristianos for your first diving experience. Not only are the waters an agreeable temperature, but the coast is sheltered from the waves and winds that can blast the northern resorts. No coral reefs, but you can expect to see barracuda, sting rays and morays among the larger fish, and shoals of trigger fish and rainbow wrasse among the smaller fry. Snorkelling is also popular.

Boat Trips

Most readers find that the dolphin and whale-watching trips are worth the euros (vegetarians may get peckish though; most include a meat-only barbecue), as you are virtually guaranteed to spot the mammals. A glass-bottom boat can add to the experience. There are several kiosks located in the harbour; the most reputable companies are listed in this chapter.

Ferries

Okay, it's not strictly a sport, but consider cruising the waters between Tenerife and La Gomera in a ferry, enjoying the view from the deck and leaving the stunning outline of El Teide behind you. You can reach here in less than an hour. La Gomera is the island that has best preserved its culture, presenting an interesting contrast to Tenerife's southern resorts.

Nearby: El Médano

Located 21km east from Los Cristianos and not yet squashed by steamroller development, El Médano is a world-class spot for wind- and kite-surfers and the sails speckle the horizon like so many exotic butterfly wings. Watersports' companies and rental outfits are mainly located near the beach, all 2km of it – the longest in Tenerife.

ALEKSANDAR TODOROVIC/SHUTTERSTOCK ©

☑ Top Tips

▶ For more watersports ideas, check out the flyers at the tourist office, ask for recommendations and visit www.todotenerife.es.

▶ Surfers will find the best waves between February and March; scuba divers the calmest waters in July and August.

▶ Look out for red flags indicating that conditions are unsafe for swimming.

✕ Take a Break

The most obvious cuisine here is seafood and one of the best places to find the flapping freshest is at the **kiosks** (Map p96, B4) on the harbour. Alternatively, El Cine (p97) offers culinary symphonies of fishy fare.

Local Life
Backstreet Los Cristianos

Step back from the tourist-clogged beachfront to discover a part of town which still has a fishing-village feel, with old-fashioned bars, idiosyncratic small shops, and an overall *pueblo* buzz with benches and squares for kickback time. Discover where the locals go for seafood and for entertainment: it's a far cry from fish and chips and karaoke.

① Bakery Breakfast

Forget about bacon and eggs and head to **Expresiones Dulces** (Calle Amalia Alayón 26, Los Cristianos; cakes from €1; ◷8am-8pm Mon-Sat), a locals' favourite where there is a mouthwatering display of cakes and pastries including such favourites as Portuguese-style custard pies, *torta de Santiago* (marzipan cake), American-style muffins and that all-time Spanish classic: churros and chocolate. Excellent coffee, too.

2 Tea Time

Or, if you're a tea drinker, stop by **La Cabaña del Té** (Calle Amalia Alayón 20, Los Cristianos; ⏱10am-8.30pm Mon-Fri), a temple to tea, its shelves filled with colourful tins of every imaginable brew, including unusual combinations like pineapple with aloe vera, *flor de cactus* (cactus flower) and banana (no surprise there!). Will also give you a cuppa while you browse.

3 Traditional Bar

Opposite the church and one of the most atmospheric and buzzing-with-locals squares in town, **Bar Gavota** (Avenida los Playeros 27, Los Cristianos; breakfast €5; ⏱8am-11pm Mon-Sat) is a perennial favourite that has retained its typical Spanish feel, as well as a faithful crowd of regulars. It's perfect for an inexpensive traditional tapa, like a generous wedge of moist tortilla, or homemade *croquetas*.

4 Craft Beers

Continue across Plaza Carmen to **Beer Shooter** (☎609 48 87 83; www.beershooter.com; Calle Juan Reveron Sierra 4, Los Cristianos; ⏱10am-2pm & 4.30-9pm Mon-Fri, to 2pm Sat), a shop plus bar which reflects the increase in the local thirst for craft beers, particularly among the 30-plus age group. There are some 250 different varieties to choose from here, including some Canary Island brews. And, forget the crisps, and go for some salty local goat cheese to accompany your ale instead. Delicious!

5 South-Coast Style

If you like bling, leopard-skin prints (on everything from Wellington boots to umbrellas), killer-heel shoes and gold lamé frocks, be sure to check out **Tina** (Calle Dulce María Loinaz 10, Los Cristianos; ⏱10am-1pm & 5-8pm Mon-Fri, 9.30am-2pm Sat). This entertainingly original boutique is reputed to have been the first to open here back in the '70s and is (and has been) frequented by generations of local *señoritas* ever since.

6 Tapas

Buzzing **La Tapa** (Calle Dulce María Loinaz, Los Cristianos; tapas €3.50; ⏱noon-midnight Wed-Mon) is much loved by locals. Appropriately (if unoriginally) named, there are 22 choices, including some traditional homestyle favourites like *callos con garbanzos* (tripe with chickpeas), *sopa de pollo* (chicken soup), plus *pescado frito* (fried seafood), *albondigas* (meatballs), potatoes with *alioli* (garlic mayonnaise)...and the list goes on.

7 Catch of the Day

Waterfront kiosk **Pescaderia Dominga** (Puerto de Los Cristianos; fish €5-9; ⏱noon-7pm Mon-Fri, to 3pm Sat) sells fresh-off-the-boat fish. You can either buy it uncooked to take away and deal with yourself, or they'll fry it up for you – and then you can dangle your legs over the edge of the nearby jetty and eat the freshest and best fish picnic you've ever had.

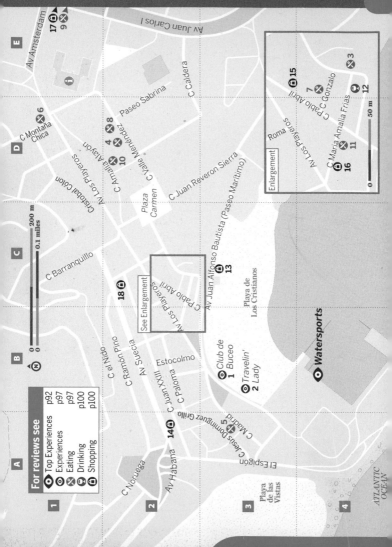

For reviews see
◉ Top Experiences   p92
◎ Experiences   p97
◯ Eating   p97
🅟 Drinking   p100
🅜 Shopping   p100

Av Amsterdam

17 🅜
9 ✕

Av Juan Carlos I

C Montaña Chica
6 ✕

Paseo Sabrina

C Caldera

15 🅜
7
3 ✕
Roma
C Pablo Abril
C Gonzalo
12 🅟
11 ✕
C María Amalia Frías
16 🅜
Av Los Playeros
Enlargement
0   50 m

C Valle Menéndez
4 ✕ 8
10
C Amalia Alayón
Av Los Playeros
Cristóbal Colón

Plaza
Carmen

C Juan Reverón Sierra

Av Juan Alfonso Bautista (Paseo Marítimo)

C Barranquillo

18 🅜

See Enlargement

Av Los Playeros
C Pablo Abril

13

Playa de
Los Cristianos

0   200 m
0   0.1 miles

N

C el Nido
C Ramón Pino
Av Suecia
Estocolmo
C Paloma
C Madrid
Club de
1 Buceo
Travelin'
2 Lady

◉ Watersports

C Noruega
Av Habana
C Juan XXIII
C Jesús Domínguez Grillo
14 🅜
5
El Espigón

Playa
de las
Vistas

ATLANTIC
OCEAN

Experiences

Club de Buceo
DIVING

1 ◎ Map p96, B3

Operates out of a kiosk in the harbour, offering a wide choice of dives, ranging from the introductory try-dive for absolute beginners. (☎922 79 73 61; www.divingaronatenerife.es; Rincon de Arona, Puerto de Los Cristianos; single dive incl equipment €60; ⊙10.30am-5pm; 👶)

Travelin' Lady
BOAT TOUR

2 ◎ Map p96, B3

Organises two-hour whale-watching trips and uses an enclosed propeller to prevent any injury to the mammals. (☎609 42 98 87; Rincon de Arona, Puerto de Los Cristianos; adult/child €18/free; ⊙9.30am-8pm Sun-Fri, noon-3pm Sat)

Eating

El Cine
SEAFOOD $

3 ✘ Map p96, E4

Yes, it's probably been said before, El Cine deserves a medal for its inexpensive, simply prepared seafood. Here since the '80s, the menu is reassuringly brief; the fish of the day is always a good bet. Tucked in an elbow off the promenade, its atmosphere of no frills and few tourists adds to the appeal. (www.barelcine.es/en; Calle Juan Bariajo 8; mains €8-10; ⊙11am-11pm)

Cultural Hotspot

The **Centro Cultural** (Map p96, E1; www.centroculturalcristiano.org; Plaza Pescador 1, Los Cristianos; ticket prices vary) equals a one-stop cultural high with art exhibitions, concerts, festivals and flamenco (aimed at locals, not tourists). If you're here for a spell, you can take a class or two: for the energetic, they range from t'ai chi to zumba and kung fu; for the more languid, patchwork to Japanese painting.

Le Bistrôt d'Alain
FRENCH $$

4 ✘ Map p96, D2

Hidden away from the masses, this formal but unassuming restaurant serves quality classic French fare such as steak with a Roquefort sauce, frogs' legs, and more unusual dishes such as a fish stew crammed with prawns, salmon and veggies. It's one of the better-regarded places to eat in town and is understandably popular with French visitors. (☎922 75 23 36; Calle Valle Menéndez 23; mains €10-15; ⊙7.30-11pm Tue-Sun)

Rincón del Marinero
SEAFOOD $$

5 ✘ Map p96, A3

Specialising in local seafood, including a tasty *zarzuela* (seafood stew), this nautical-themed restaurant has all its tables under a covered terrace (proof that there's never bad weather here). (Muelle Los Cristianos, Los Cristianos; mains €9-15; ⊙noon-11pm)

Top Tip

Swimming

In general swimming here is safe, however, even the calmest waters can be subject to an undertow which is often no more than 10 metres wide. If you are drawn into an undertow, don't make the common mistake of trying to swim back to shore against the tide; instead, turn 90 degrees and swim parallel to the coastline.

It is perfectly okay to go topless on the beaches and around the hotel pools here (unless otherwise specified). At the other extreme, you should cover up if you are visiting a church here; no mini skirts, shorts or bare midriffs.

Sopa   VEGETARIAN $

6   Map p96, D1

A chilled-out space with sofas, books and magazines provides the backdrop for a menu of healthy soups, salads and burgers (spinach, that is). There are also delicious cakes. Try the cherry and marzipan for a real tastebud treat. (Calle Montaña Chica 2; salads & soups €4-7; ⏰8am-9pm Mon-Sat, 9am-9pm Sun; 🛜🍴🚻)

The Original Bistro   BISTRO $$

7   Map p96, E4

Run by a Spanish-English couple, this enormously popular bistro offers a three-course menu with several choices. You won't find any foam or drizzle here; dishes are homely and (mainly) traditionally British – but executed with finesse with not an overboiled veg in sight. (☎922 79 20 31; Callejón Gonzalo; mains €10-12; ⏰6-11pm Wed-Mon; 🚻)

Restaurante Fortuna Nova   SPANISH $$

8   Map p96, D2

The food is classically Spanish and, considering the price, is of a very high standard. There's a nice shady terrace to eat on and it's popular at lunchtime with local workers, which is always a good sign. (Calle Valle Menéndez; mains €10-12; ⏰noon-4pm & 6-11pm; 🚻)

La Pepa Food Market   MARKET $

9   Map p96, E1

This gourmet food market opened in 2015 and is still expanding. At the time of research there were some 25 stalls including upmarket delis, seafood counter, pancakes and waffles stand, sushi, a wine bar and a vegetarian snack stall. There is plenty of seating on a vast terrace with rooftop views that stretch to the sea, plus a children's playground. (☎922 79 48 85; www.mercadolapepa.es; Centro Comercial La Pasarela; snacks €2.50-5; ⏰10am-11pm Mon-Thu, to midnight Fri-Sun; 🅿🛜🍴🚻)

Tasca Nano   TAPAS $

10   Map p96, D2

This is a no-frills earthy bar that serves tapas like black pudding (and you can't get much more earthy than

Rincón del Marinero (p97)

that...). The house wine is palatable and the atmosphere convivial. Feeling chummy? Then get a *ración* of *patatas bravas* (fried potatoes in a spicy tomato sauce) to share. (Calle Amalia Alayón 6; tapas €2-4.50; ⊘8am-11pm Mon-Fri, 10am-4pm Sat)

Riva Dulce   ICE CREAM $

11 ✕ Map p96, D4

There is nothing bubble-gum flavoured or flash about this diminutive ice-cream place one street back from the beach, which is more like just a counter. But the Italian ice cream is, well Italian, so it's about the best in town. (Calle Dulce María Loinaz 3; cone €2.50; ⊘11am-3pm & 5-10pm)

Understand
Island of Dogs

Look out for the native island dog here. Known as Verdino, it is powerful and smooth haired with Rottweiler-style wide jaws. The name comes from the colour, which is slightly greenish. Some people believe that the Canary Islands were named after these native dogs (*canis* in Latin), which date back to the time of the Guanches, who kept them to guard their flocks. These days they are kept as pets.

IAN SHAW/ALAMY ©

Top Tip

Top Tipples

Ditch the G&T and opt for a mojito or caipirinha cocktail. Based on local rum, made from cane sugar, they are a reminder of the island's Latin American connections and are generally authentic (and addictive!).

Drinking

Beach House BAR

12 🔍 Map p96, E4

This Italian-run bar has a classy feel with its chill-out music, pale-grey paintwork, candy-coloured cushions and TV switched to the fashion (rather than football) channel. Good for cocktails. (Paseo Dulce María Lenaz; ⊘5pm-late; 🛜)

Shopping

La Alpizpa CRAFTS

13 🔒 Map p96, C3

Located right on the seafront, this shop sells high-quality and diverse arts and crafts created by people with disabilities. (Paseo Marítimo; ⊘10am-2pm & 5-7pm Mon-Sat)

Jamón y Mojo FOOD & DRINK

14 🔒 Map p96, A2

Run by an enthusiastic young couple, this deli has a vast range of carefully

sourced gourmet products with an emphasis on such Spanish delights as great wheels of crumbly Manchego cheese and several grades of chorizo and *jamón serrano*. They also make superb sandwiches using speciality breads and carry an extensive selection of wines. (🖉674 73 60 01; www. jamonymojo.es; Avenida Suecia 35; ⊘10am-9pm Mon-Sat)

Librería Barbara BOOKS

15 🔒 Map p96, E3

Founded in 1984 and selling a wide range of books in several languages including English, French, German and Spanish, plus magazines and children's titles. (🖉922 79 23 01; Calle Pablo Abril 6; ⊘10am-1pm & 5-7.30pm Mon-Fri, 10am-1pm Sat)

Top Tip

Scams

If you get offered a scratchcard along with a potential free gift, turn it down and walk away, saying something like 'I *never* play scratchcards!' Every card that you are offered on the promenade has one potential outcome: a timeshare rip off.

Also don't be tempted by so-called free coach tours, generally touted via leaflets distributed on the street. They will always involve a persuasive sales pitch for some product or other which is generally overpriced and of poor quality.

Pesquera y Navales Tenerife

SPORTS

16 🔒 Map p96, D4

If you fancy dropping a line and sinker, or investing in some thigh-high wellies (in secret or otherwise), or just browsing through the piled high shelves of every imaginable product, item of clothing or seafaring souvenir related to that catch of the day, then this is the shop for you. (📞922 79 91 11; Calle Dulce María Loinaz 1; 🕙10am-1.30pm Mon-Fri, to 1.30pm Sat)

Olé Espacio Gourmet

FOOD & DRINK

17 🔒 Map p96, E1

A temple to all things gastronomic with an emphasis on Canarian products like *mojo* sauces, local goat's cheese and herb-infused honey. Also sells one of the most highly regarded *jamones serranos* in the world, the Cinco Jotas Sanchez Romero Carvajal. (La Pepa Food Market stand 21-22, Centro Comercial La Pasarela; 🕙10am-11pm; 📶)

Blazers

FASHION

18 🔒 Map p96, C2

A refreshing change from the humdrum fashions aimed at souvenir-

Playa de Los Cristianos (p92)

hoarding tourists (like slogan blazoned T-shirts and overpriced swimwear), this eye-catching boutique has a fun youthful edge with its collection of slinky dresses with intricate lacework, as well as more informal wear. (📞922 79 31 94; Calle Juan XXIII; 🕙10.30am-1.30pm & 5-8.30pm Mon-Sat)

Explore

Playa de las Américas & Costa Adeje

It's easy to get sniffy about Playa de las Américas and, while its reputation for sun-kissed holidays for the masses is well earned, it's not what it used to be. True, the resort is still 100% tourist driven, but there is a sophisticated sheen to the place now which is especially evident in the bars, restaurants and overall nightlife that seem to merge seamlessly with the adjacent, upmarket Costa Adeje.

The Sights in a Day

☀ Start your day with a coffee on the terrace at **Bar el Pincho** (p113) overlooking Playa de las Vistas (great for hair-of-the-dog cocktails as well!). Then head to **Aqua Marina** (p106) to find out about their range of family-friendly diving courses. Next stop is the tourist office to find out what is going on in town; there's usually plenty.

☀ Time for a spot of retail enter-tainment and there's lots of window-shopping choice (and space for strolling) on Avenida Rafael Puig Lluvina. Slow down with traditional tapas at **Meson Las Lanzas** (p112), then drop down to the beach and continue to **Artenerife** (p114) to check out fine art and crafts.

☾ Walk or taxi it to the Costa Adeje (pictured left) to take some spa time out at **Aequor Spa** (p107), one of several luxurious spas in these parts. Duly relaxed, extend your chill-out time at appealing **Café La Bahia** (p110), followed by a mojito on the beach at **Chiringuito del Mirador** (p113). Staying in these parts, do a spot of shopping at bijou **Centro Comercial El Mirador** (p114), followed by dinner at **Ocanto** (p111) overlooking the waves.

♥ Best of Playa de las Américas

Eating
The Oriental Monkey (p109)

Thai Botanico (p109)

Christy's (p110)

Chunga Changa (p110)

Drinking
Bar el Pincho (p113)

Hard Rock Cafe (p112)

Kiosco San Telmo (p113)

Beaches
Playa de las Vistas (p106)

Playa del Duque (p106)

Spas
Mare Nostrum (p106)

Getting There

🚌 **Bus** Plenty of TITSA buses come through the area, stopping at Playa de las Américas. Buses 110 (direct, €9.70, one hour, every 30 minutes) and 111 (indirect) come and go from Santa Cruz. Bus 343 (€3.70, 45 minutes) goes to Tenerife Sur airport. For comprehensive bus information, visit www.titsa.com.

Autopista Sur

Siam Park

Av Pueblos

Av de Austria

Parque de San Eugenio

Av Centenario

Paseo Marítimo

Barranco del Rey

Av Rafael Puig Lluvina

⌂ 23, 25
⌂ 30, 32

◉ 2, 7
✕ 14, 17

Ola Diving
Center

✕ 15

✕ 16

❷ 21

❷ 31 ⌂

❷ 20

Av de Colón

COSTA
ADEJE 9

Neptuno ◉ 10

Playa de
Torviscas

Playa
del
Bobo

Playa de Troya

ATLANTIC
OCEAN

Experiences

Playa de las Vistas
BEACH

1 ◎ Map p104, D8

A sublime 1.5km long beach with fine golden sand (imported from the Sahara Desert!), linking Los Cristianos with Playa de las Américas. The beach is backed by bars and restaurants and protected by breakwaters, so perfect for swimming. (Playa de las Américas)

Playa del Duque
BEACH

2 ◎ Map p104

Appropriately named, the 600m-long Duke's beach is an appealing golden-sandy stretch backed by jaunty striped changing huts, chic cafes and restaurants. (Costa Adeje)

☑ Top Tip

Costa Adeje

Keep walking north from Playa de las Américas and the avenues become wider, the landscaping is lusher, the hotels grander.... This is an area that has worked hard to revamp its image, gradually shifting to an increasingly upmarket resort. Wide boulevards are studded with flower beds and flanked by lofty palms; HP sauce is being usurped by pomegranate balsamic; and shops are increasingly designer-label conscious. Costa Adeje is the glitzier end of the playa, home to southern Tenerife's most sophisticated places to eat, drink and play.

Mare Nostrum
SPA

3 ◎ Map p104, C7

Part of this major resort in Playa de las Américas and sure to spoil. There are those enticing-sounding fungal wraps and electrotherapy for serious spa-goers, plus massages and steam baths for those seeking to de-stress. (☑ 922 75 75 45; www.marenostrumspa. es; Avenida de las Américas, Playa de las Américas; ⊙ 10am-7pm)

Aqua Marina
DIVING

4 ◎ Map p104, C8

Offers the standard array of boat dives, courses and speciality dives as well as plain old snorkelling for those who don't want to get their hair wet. Also runs bubblemaker courses for children. (☑ 922 79 79 44; www.aquama rinadivingtenerife.com; Playa de las Vistas, Playa de las Américas; single dive €39, kids bubblemaker course €35; ⊙ 9am-6pm; ﹢)

Arona Tenerife Surf Academy
SURFING

5 ◎ Map p104, B5

The only surf school handily located right on the beach. The instructors are licensed by the Canarian Surf Federation and offer courses on a choice of boards ranging from shortboards to standup paddle boards. Wetsuit gear available to rent. (☑ 665 01 75 78; www. aronatenerifesurf.com; Playa Honda, Playa de las Américas; 2hr lesson incl equipment from €35)

DARIOSA44/GETTY IMAGES ©

Playa del Duque

K-16 Surf
SURFING

6 ⊙ Map p104, B7

Rents out surfboards and provides tuition for only slightly more than the price of rental. (☏922 79 84 80; www. k16surf.com; Calle México 1-2, Playa de las Américas; surf lessons from €35, board rental per day from €12)

Aequor Spa
SPA

7 ⊙ Map p104, B1

Part of the fabulous Hotel Jardines de Nivaria, the Aequor Spa can get you in the mood for a little self pampering with a range of treatments and massages plus a ritual spa experi-ence complete with Bach flowers and minerals (€150 euros for 90 minutes). Pure bliss! (Hotel Jardines de Nivaria; www. adrianhoteles.com; Calle Paris, Playa de Fañabé, Costa Adeje; ⊙10am-7pm Mon-Sat)

Itaka Diving
DIVING

8 ⊙ Map p104, D8

A long-established diving centre with PADI-recognised courses ranging from Open Water Diver to Divemaster, plus single dives for beginners and multiple-dive packages. (☏922 78 80 85; www.itakadiving.com; edificio Cristianos 111, local A4, Avenida Habana, Playa de las Américas; single dive incl equipment €35)

Understand
A Brief History of Tenerife

The Guanches
The first people to live here were the aboriginal Guanches, who were persecuted and driven out by waves of marauding invaders. Thought to be related to the Berbers of North Africa, how they arrived here is a mystery as they apparently possessed no boats.

Conquests & Affluence
The first major conquest of the island was by French adventurer, Jean de Béthencourt in the 15th century. He was backed by the Spanish Catholic monarchs who had already taken Granada on the mainland. With the discovery of the New World, Tenerife became a wealthy trading post, first for sugar and subsequently grapes, which were used for producing Malmsey wine, then considered to be the best in the world. This wealthy period of history is reflected in the grandiose colonial-style buildings in La Laguna and La Orotava. Spain's control of the islands didn't go unchallenged. The most spectacular success went to Admiral Robert Blake, under Cromwell, who annihilated a Spanish treasure fleet at Santa Cruz. British harassment culminated in 1797 with Admiral Nelson's attack on the city, when he not only failed to storm the town but lost his right arm in the fighting.

Economic Woes
The Canaries were declared a province of Spain in 1821 and Santa Cruz de Tenerife was made the capital. The economic fallout from the Spanish Civil War and World War II plunged the islands into economic misery. Many Canarios opted to emigrate, including 16,000 who headed for Venezuela, one third of whom perished in the ocean crossings.

The Onset of Tourism
Not until the 1960s did the economy start to pick up with the onset of tourism to the islands, particularly from the UK and Germany. In 1978 Tenerife opened the Reina Sofía airport in the south, which concurrently led to the mass development of the Playa de las Américas. Today close to 85% of all tourists head for the southern resorts, although the percentages are gradually shifting as more visitors discover the quieter, greener and more traditional side of the island in the interior and the north.

Ola Diving Center DIVING

9 Map p104, B2

Offers possibly the most extensive choice of diving courses in the region, including recreational, technical and cave diving. They also organise diving seminars, as well as courses from beginners to instructor level. Boat trips to Masca also arranged (four hours, €53). (822 66 48 76; www.ola-aventura.com; Avenida de Colón, Costa Adeje; 9am-5pm)

Neptuno BOAT TOUR

10 Map p104, B2

This reputable company organises several boat tours, incuding a 5-hour excursion on a traditional sailing ship (formerly owned by a sheikh) where you're almost guaranteed to see dolphins and whales, and which includes an option to swim in the bay of Masca and enjoy a traditional paella lunch. Complimentary hotel shuttle service available. (922 79 80 44; www.barcostenerife.com; Calle Colon S/N, Puerto Colon; 5-hour boat tour adult/child €49/24; 9am-9pm)

Eating

The Oriental Monkey ASIAN $$$

11 Map p104, B1

Voted top Canary Island international restaurant in 2013 and with celebrated chef Nacho Hernández at the helm, this gourmet restaurant combines exotic decor with an exotic menu of innovatively prepared Asian-inspired dishes, ranging from marinated cod in miso, to tuna *tataki* with smoked aubergine and couscous. (922 78 92 91; www.theoriental-monkey.com; Avenida de las Américas, Central Comercial Oasis, Playa de las Américas; mains €18-25; 7-11pm Mon-Sat;)

Thai Botanico THAI $$

12 Map p104, B7

This enchanting place sparks on all cylinders with sumptuous oriental decor and beautifully crafted Thai dishes. Curries, stir fries, salads, spring rolls and satay dishes...all the Thai favourites are here, delicately enhanced by fragrant herbs and

---

Understand
Las Galletas

This charming small resort has a long history as a fishing village, stretching back to before the Spanish conquest. Despite being just a few kilometres south of the Las Américas' strip, it has a tranquil ambience, together with a largely Canarian populace and overall lack of multistorey hotels and tourists. The small marina is fronted by a boardwalk lined with bars and restaurants, including some good seafood choices. Arrive early, and you might just see the fishermen selling their daily catch. Las Galletas is also considered one of the best diving spots in southern Tenerife; several diving schools offer opportunities to take the plunge. Or you might just want to lounge on the pleasant beach!

Top Tip

Know Your South-Coast Beaches

Tenerife's south-coast beaches come complete with mojito-mixing beach bars and chic restaurants; some of the best include golden-sand Playa de las Vistas (p106), family-friendly Playa de Los Cristianos (p92) and chic Playa del Duque (p106). For something more low-key, head to the beaches at the nearby towns of Las Galletas (p109) and El Médano (p93).

spices. Reservations essential. (☏ 922 79 77 59; www.thaibotanicotenerife.com; Avenida Américas, Playa de Las Américas; mains €12-14; ☺ 1.30-11.30pm Mon-Sat, 5-11pm Sun; 🛜)

Gastrobar La Kocina   CONTEMPORARY SPANISH $$

13 ✕ Map p104, D7

A slick contemporary interior is the appropriate setting for enjoying pretty-as-a-picture tapas served on black-slate platters. Enticingly diverse dishes may include earthy wild mushrooms with garlic and parsley, suckling pig and tuna *tataki*, with the menu changing according to what is fresh in the market that day. (☏ 922 79 46 30; Avenida Antonio Domínguéz, Playa de las Américas; tapas €8-15; ☺ noon-4pm & 7.30-11.30pm; 🛜)

Café La Bahia   CAFE $$

14 ✕ Map p104, B1

Don't miss the Playa del Duque; one of most picturesque golden-sand beaches in southern Tenerife. Draw up a chair at this French Riviera–feel cafe with its giant sun umbrellas, Med-blue tablecloths and waiters wearing boaters, then choose between a coffee, *cerveza* (beer) or ice cream. Light meals also available. (Playa del Duque, Costa Adeje; mains €12-15; ☺ 9am-6pm)

Christy's   BRITISH $

15 ✕ Map p104, B3

It's easy to get sniffy about all the British-grub places here, but if you secretly fancy going for a Sunday roast and Yorkshire pud or beer-battered cod with homemade chips, this Scottish-owned bar and restaurant offers superb quality and huge portions. There's a small outside terrace and large dining room appropriately decorated with pics of London buses and similar for homesick Brits. (☏ 922 79 83 01; Avenida Eugenio Domínguéz, Costa Adeje; mains €7-9; ☺ 11am-11pm Wed-Mon)

Chunga Changa   ITALIAN $

16 ✕ Map p104, C4

Run by an enthusiastic young Italian team, this place is a bit of an institution here: especially at sunset happy-hour time when cocktails drop to €3.50, a hiccup of a price in these parts. They will also organise a picnic,

Thai Botanico (p109)

not just providing the food, but also the towels and sunscreen. Homemade pasta made with spelt, rice salads, strawberry and feta-cheese 'kebabs'; the food is fun and creative. (☏922 09 33 36; Avenida Rafael Puig Lluvina, Costa Adeje; mains €7-10; ☺11.30am-11.30pm)

Ocanto
CONTEMPORARY CANARIAN **$$**

17 ✕ Map p104, B1

If all that credit-card swiping in the surrounding boutiques has worked up a thirst, stop by this enticing bar which combines classy dark-wicker furniture with a sumptuous plant-filled terrace overlooking the waves. Enjoy light bites to share, like salmon tartar with avocado and fried squid topped with a coriander-spiked aioli. (Avenida Bruselas, Costa Adeje; mains €11-20; ☺11am-1am; ☎)

El Faro
MODERN CANARIAN **$$$**

18 ✕ Map p104, B7

For a swanky night out, El Faro fits the bill (although we must say that the fake lighthouse, which lends its name to the restaurant, is naff in the extreme). Watch the world go by from the 2nd-storey terrace as you savour the imaginatively prepared meat, fish and pasta dishes. (☏922 75 38 27; Avenida Américas, Parque Santiago V, Playa de las Américas; mains €20-25; ☺noon-4pm & 7-11pm)

Meson Las Lanzas SPANISH $$

19 Map p104, C6

Hurray. No sunbleached photos of chips-with-everything 'international' dishes on the pavement. Instead come here to enjoy traditional Spanish mains like *tigres* (deep-fried mussels) and roast shoulder of lamb. The preparation is simplicity itself, just fresh and homely cuisine; don't miss it. (☏922 79 11 72; www.mesonlaslanzas.es; Avenida Noelia Alfonso Cabrera 8, Playa de las Américas; mains €14-19; ☺1-4pm & 7pm-midnight)

Drinking

Papagayo BAR, CLUB

20 Map p104, B4

This restaurant, bar and nightclub oozes sophistication and good taste. The decor is predominantly white, with kick-back seating, shady canopies and water features, while the menu is best for light dishes like sushi. Come night time the place metamorphoses into a fashionable nightclub, complete with a slick professional DJ and dancers. (www.papagayobeachclub.com; Playa de Troya, Avenida Rafael Puig Lluvina, Playa de las Américas; ☺10am-late; �awifi)

Monkey Beach Club CLUB

21 Map p104, C4

Right on the beachfront at Playa de Troya, this is a winning spot for a sundowner which gradually fills up

with a hip good-looking crowd who gather here to drink, flirt and dance on the strobe-lit dancefloor. Some turn up earlier for a bite to eat. (☏922 78 92 91; www.grupomonkey.com; Avenida Rafael Puig Lluvina 3, Playa de las Américas; ☺10.30am-late; ☎wifi)

Hard Rock Cafe BAR

22 Map p104, C7

Part of the worldwide rock 'n' roll chain with a buzzy vibe, music-themed decor and a stunning rooftop terrace with sea views beyond the palms. Live acoustic music on Wednesdays and occasional concerts throughout the year; check the website for the line up. (☏922 05 50 22; www.hardrock.com; Avenida Américas, Playa de las Américas; ☺12.30pm-1.30am Mon-Fri, to 3am Fri & Sat; ☎wifi)

Understand
Half-Board Headache

Bars and restaurants in these parts are seriously suffering, as hotels here are increasingly offering half-board all-inclusive deals to their guests at cheap-as-chips prices. Hotel buffets are typically based on bland international cuisine aimed at appealing to the masses.

Chiringuito del Mirador BAR

23 Map p104, B1

This beach bar (and restaurant) has a sparkling summer-in-the-sun feel, with its glossy white furniture and decor contrasting with the deep blue of the sea, just a few metres away. It's a lovely place for a midday cocktail or *cerveza,* accompanied by a plate of *gambas a la plancha* (grilled prawns) to share. (Playa del Duque, Costa Adeje; ⊙noon-7pm)

Dubliner IRISH PUB

24 Map p104, B6

This place has a suitably blarney atmosphere, together with Guinness on tap and nightly live music provided by the accomplished and popular resident band. (☏922 79 39 03; Hotel Las Palmeras, Avenida Rafael Puig Lluvina, Playa de las Américas; ⊙9pm-5am; 🖥)

Chiringuito Coqueluche BAR

25 Map p104, B1

Stroll along the promenade, past luxurious hotel gardens and around a small headland to the attractive dark-pebble beach of La Enramada, where you can sip a drink with sand between your toes at the cheerful local beach bar and watch the paragliders drift on by. (Playa La Enramada, Costa Adeje; ⊙10am-7pm)

Local Life
Kiosco San Telmo

The antithesis of the brash drinking dens that still exist in these parts, **Kiosco San Telmo** (Playa de las Vistas, Playa de las Américas; ⊙10am-7pm) is a simple wooden kiosk on Playa de las Vistas, which happily has all the necessary to whip up a killer mojito, which you can sip on a stool while scuffing the sand.

Bar El Pincho BAR

26 Map p104, D8

Come here for a cocktail at sunset; the mango daiquiris are the ideal accompaniment to the uninterrupted sand-and-sea views from the terrace above the boardwalk. Tapas also served. (☏922 79 77 19; www.barelpincho.com; Playa de las Vistas, Playa de las Américas; ⊙10.30am-9pm Mon-Sat)

Akustito COCKTAIL BAR

27 Map p104, B7

It's little more than a shack on the beach but the mojitos are advertised as being the best in the world and, much like their Cuban counterparts, they are certainly cracking (and strong). On Saturdays there's a live band; at other times, chill-out music sets the scene nicely. (☏616 25 17 68; Paseo Marítimo, Playa de las Américas; mojitos €5; ⊙noon-late)

Top Tip

Don't Speed!

Speed cameras are on the increase and are now commonplace on the island. Watch the speed limit at all times as they can vary considerably, even on a short stretch of road. Fines are in the region of €100 and you often have to pay up on the spot.

Entertainment

La Pirámide
LIVE MUSIC

28 ⭐ Map p104, C7

This vast auditorium (one of the largest in Europe) regularly stages world-class shows that typically combine flamenco, opera and dance. There is an option to combine the show with a buffet dinner (from €75) with dining times set at 6.30pm and 7pm. However, by all reports, the food is decidedly less impressive than the show. (📞922 75 75 49; www.piramidearona.com; La Pirámide, Avenida Américas, Playa de las Américas; tickets from €50; ⏰8pm Wed, 9pm Tue, Thu-Sun)

Sax Bar
LIVE MUSIC

29 ⭐ Map p104, B6

If you like to rock and are not averse to a mainly British clientele, then Sax may just well be your nightly boogy fix. The resident bands are up there with the best; you can even have a warble yourself – there's a karaoke slot post midnight. (📞680 83 14 88; Calle Mexico, Playa de las Américas; ⏰9pm-late)

Shopping

Centro Comercial El Mirador
SHOPPING CENTRE

30 🔒 Map p104, B1

Near the main sweep of beach on the Costa Adeje is this bijou shopping centre, with boutiques set around prettily tiled patios and fountains with palms, arches and pots of brilliant-red geraniums. Fittingly overlooked by the meandering gardens and jasmine-flanked paths of the El Mirador hotel, the small independently owned shops here sell everything from designer swimwear to handmade wooden toys. (www.el-mirador.es; Avenida Bruselas, Costa Adeje; ⏰10am-9pm Mon-Sat)

Artenerife
CRAFTS

31 🔒 Map p104, B4

Part of an island-wide chain where quality control is very much in evidence, Artenerife carries a superb range of quality handicrafts originating in the Canary Islands. (www.artenerife. com; Avenida Rafael Puig Lluvina, Playa de las Américas; ⏰9.30am-1.30pm & 5-7pm Mon-Sat)

Plaza del Duque
COMMERCIAL CENTRE

32 🔒 Map p104, B1

A luxurious small shopping centre with around 60 shops, including designer boutiques and a kids zone. (www.plazadelduque.com; Playa del Duque, Costa Adeje; ⏰10am-7pm Mon-Fri, to 2pm Sat; 📶🎫)

Centro Comercial El Mirador

Paku's
FASHION

Located in Hotel Las Palmeras (see **24** Map p104, B6), Paku's sells stylish men's fashions in bright jazzy patterns and colours catering to a wide range of sizes from extra small to extra large. (☑922 78 73 95; Hotel Las Palmeras, Avenida de Rafael Puig Lluvina, Playa de las Américas; ◷10am-7pm)

Hensi
SHOES

33 🔒 Map p104, C5

If you like to stride (or strut) out in quality eye-catching shoes, you will love this shoe shop, which stocks all those designer name brands, including Boss, Tommy Hilfiger, Diesel, Ralph Lauren and Armani. (☑922 79 89 88; www.hensi.es; Avenida Rafael Puig Lluvina 5, Playa de las Américas)

Bounty
FASHION

34 🔒 Map p104, B7

Not the kind of place you want to enter with sand between your toes, this exclusive boutique sells quality traditional and contemporary fashions for men and women, featuring designer names (and not), as well as a limited and exclusive range of pretty shoes and accessories. (☑922 28 82 11; Avenida Américas 56, Playa de las Américas; ◷10am-7pm Mon-Fri, to 2pm Sat)

Top Experiences
Parque Nacional del Teide

🚌 Just two public buses arrive at the park daily: bus 348 from Puerto de la Cruz (€6.20, one hour) and bus 342 from Los Cristianos (€7, 1½ hours).

Standing sentry over Tenerife, formidable El Teide is, at a whopping 3718m, the highest mountain in all Spain and is, in every sense of the word, the highlight of a trip to Tenerife. The surrounding national park covers 189.9 sq km, encompassing the volcano and the surrounding hinterland, and is both a Unesco World Heritage site and Spain's most popular national park. The area is truly extraordinary, comprising a haunting lunar moonscape of surreal rock formations, mystical caves and craggy peaks.

Don't Miss

Self-Guided Walks

The visitor guide lists 21 walks, varying in length from 600m to a strenuous 17.6km, some of which are signposted. Each walk is graded according to its level of difficulty. You are not allowed to stray from the marked trails, a sensible restriction in an environment where every tuft of plant life has to fight for survival.

Most Spectacular Hike

A fabulous hike is to climb to the summit of **Pico Viejo,** then walk along the ridge that connects this mountain to Teide and on up to the summit. Allow nine hours (one way) and be prepared to walk back down Teide again if the cable car is closed. Consider staying overnight at the **Refugio de Altavista** (☎902 67 86 76; Cañadas del Teide, Parque Nacional del Teide; dm €21) at 3270m.

Guided Hikes

Park rangers host free guided walks around the mountain in both Spanish and English. The pace is gentle and even though you'll huff and puff rather more than usual because of the high altitude, the walks are suitable for anyone of reasonable fitness, including older kids. Groups leave at 9.15am and 1.30pm from El Portillo (p117) visitor centre; advance reservations essential.

Roques de Garcia

A few kilometres south of El Teide peak, across from the *parador*, lies this extraordinary geological formation of twisted lava pinnacles with names like the Finger of God and the Cathedral. They are the result of the erosion of old volcanic dykes, or vertical streams of magma. A family-friendly trail leads around the Roques, where you won't need more than comfortable shoes and

El Portillo Visitors Centre

☎922 92 37 71

www.reservasparques
nacionales.es

Carretera La Orotava–Granadilla

🕑9am-4pm

☑ Top Tips

▶ Avoid taking the cable car if you suffer from altitude sickness; walking and taking your time will help with acclimatisation.

▶ Take warm clothing, as El Teide is far cooler than the rest of the island.

✗ Take a Break

The **Parador Nacional** (☎922 37 48 41; www.parador.es; d incl breakfast €145; P❊🛜🏊) inside the park has an excellent, elegant restaurant. Alternatively, head to **Vilaflor** where there's more eating choices, including **El Rincon de Roberto** (☎922 70 90 35; Avenida Hermano Pedro 27; mains €12-18; 🕑noon-5pm Mon, to 10pm Wed-Sat), specialising in slow-cooked Canarian cuisine.

Top Tip

For any of the longer routes, you'll need proper walking boots, plus poles, some food, a map and a compass. Don't underestimate El Teide: it may not be the Himalayas, but it's still a serious mountain.

some warm clothing. Spreading out to the west are the otherworldly bald plains of the Llano de Ucanca.

Cable Car to the Summit

The **cable car** (☎922 01 04 40; www. telefericoteide.com; cable car adult/child €26/13; ☺9am-4pm; P) provides the easiest, and most popular way to reach the El Teide peak. On clear days, the volcanic peak spreads out majestically below and you can see the islands of La Gomera, La Palma and El Hierro peeking up from the Atlantic. It takes just eight minutes to zip up 1200m. Bring a jacket – and a camera.

Climbing the Peak

If you plan on climbing to the summit of El Teide you must reserve your place online at www.reservasparques nacionel.es. You can reserve up to 2pm the day before you want to climb and choose from several two-hour slots per day in which to make your final ascent to the summit. In addition to the permit, take along your passport or ID.

Observatorio del Teide

One of the best places in the northern hemisphere to stargaze is the **Observatorio del Teide**. Scientists come from the world over to study here. You can have a free tour, but need to make an appointment first. For more information, check out www.iac.es. **Volcano Life Experience** (☎922 01 04 44; www. volcanolife.com; tour €30), a private tour company, also offer a number of stargazing packages starting from €30 per person.

Understand
Pico Viejo

El Teide was considered a sacred site by the Guanches, who famously believed it held up the sky. The volcano has erupted several times since the island was colonised in 1402, including four times in the 18th century and, most recently, in 1909. In 1789, its southwestern flank tore open leaving a 700m gash. Today you can clearly see where fragments of magma shot over 1km into the air and fell pell-mell. To this day, not a blade of grass or stain of lichen has returned to the arid slope. Although it is currently dormant, many scientists believe it may blow in the near future.

Pico Viejo

Appreciating the Geology

The national park area is protected, fortunately, as it contains 14 plants found nowhere else in the world, including the delicate Teide daisy. The park is also geologically fascinating; of the many different types of volcanic formations found in the world, examples of more than 80% can be found here, as well as complex formations like volcanic pipes and cones.

Nearby: Vilaflor

Located on the sunny southern flanks of El Teide, Vilaflor claims to be the highest village in Spain, at an altitude of 1400m. Head for the main square where all the places of interest are located, including shops selling local lacework, and traditional bars and restaurants. Duck into the 16th-century parish church, as well, which honours Tenerife's one and only saint: San Pedro.

Nearby: Santiago del Teide

This small town, sitting just to the northwest of the national park boundary makes a superb base for visiting Los Gigantes, Garachico and Masca; the latter is one of the most spectacular villages in Tenerife, teetering on the very brink of a knife-edge ridge and surrounded by the beautiful Parque Rural de Teno – great for hiking.

Local Life
Village Life in Garachico

🚌 107 connects the town with Santa Cruz (€8.15, two hours), La Laguna and La Orotava and bus 363 with Puerto de la Cruz (€3.75, one hour, up to 20 daily).

This gracious, tranquil town is located in a deep valley flanked by forested slopes and a rocky coastline. Often bypassed by tourists, Garachico has managed to retain its intrinsic Canarian identity; spend a few hours here, exploring the quaint cobbled streets, dipping into local tapas bars and absorbing the traditional culture and lifestyle.

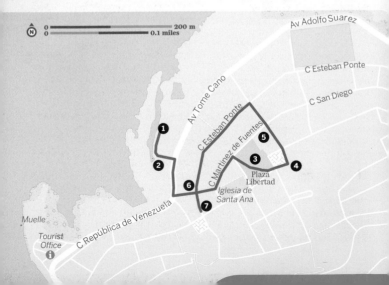

❶ Volcanic Coves

Strung along the seafront these natural pools and channels are known as **El Caletón** (Avenida Tome Cano) and were formed by the lava flow from a volcanic eruption in 1706, which buried half the town. Today they are ideal for paddling toddlers or swimming; some are even deep enough for diving. It's a fascinating and unique spot.

❷ Waterfront Amble

Wander along the rocky-cove waterfront, past local fishermen waiting for a bite, dropping by the **Castillo de San Miguel** (Avenida Tome Cano; adult/child €2/ free; ☉10am-4pm), which contains a modest two-room museum about the history of the town, including exhibits on piracy, sealife and geology. Climb the tower for the best views.

❸ Sitting in the Square

Stroll through one of Tenerife's prettiest plazas, **Plaza Libertad**, where old men in flat caps play cards or dominoes surrounded by sauntering couples, children kicking balls and families shaded by Indian laurel trees. The kiosk-cum-cafe here serves coffee, drinks and snacks and there's a wonderful view of the adjacent 16th-century church.

❹ Pondering on the Past

On the corner of the plaza sits the gracious 16th-century **Convento de San Francisco** (Plaza Libertad; adult/child €2/ free; ☉11am-2pm & 3-6pm Mon-Fri, 10am-4pm Sat). This rambling museum has exhibits set around beautiful cloisters, which include the volcanic history of the town and islands and some fascinating early-20th-century photos of the town, complete with resident camels.

❺ Tapa Time

Passing the sumptuous Hotel La Quinta Roja, double round the back to the delightful small bar **Tasca de Vino** (☎696 69 52 75; Glorieta de San Francisco; tapa plus drink €2.50; ☉noon-4pm & 7-11pm), located on a picturesque cobbled sidestreet and where you can enjoy a drink with a generous portioned tapa for the euro-economising price of just €2.50.

❻ Potty about Pottery

Near here is a ceramic and art shop, which would look happily at home in any urban-chic big city. Run by German artist Alice Gauer and her Spanish partner Julian Betemps, **Art Shop** (www.artshop-garachico.com; Calle Esteban Ponte 3; ☉11am-8pm) has an eclectic display of art, including sea urchin jewellery, carved wooden plates, contemporary ceramics, and paintings.

❼ Traditional Tasca

Wind up your day at wonderful **Casa Ramón** (Calle Esteban de Ponte 4; mains €6-8; ☉1-8pm Mon-Sat), a tapas bar run by an elderly lady who refuses to make any concessions to the modern age; bills are written on scraps of paper and coffee is unheard of. The food is mainly local seafood and varies daily.

Local Life
Exploring the Anaga Mountains

Getting There

🚗 Your own vehicle is the best way to explore this region.

🚌 Limited bus services link Santa Cruz to Taganana via San Andrés, six times daily (€1.60, 50 minutes).

These stunning rugged mountains are home to centuries' old laurel forests, pine-clad mountains, tiny unspoiled villages and emerald-green valleys. They sprawl across the far northeast corner of the island and offer some of the most spectacular scenery in Tenerife. Unsurprisingly, this is one of the best regions for hiking on the island.

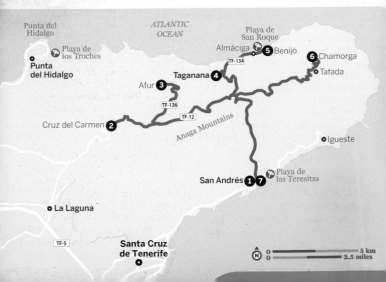

❶ Breakfast by the Beach

Head to San Andrés, its narrow shady streets lined with fishers' cottages. Grab a coffee at **Bar El Peton** (☏922 59 11 29; Calle Aparejo; mains €7-9; ⏱7am-7pm) and perch at one of its five tables. Then stroll to the end of the promenade to admire the sweeping arc of white sand that is Playa de las Teresitas, arguably the most beautiful beach in Tenerife.

❷ Cruz del Carmen

The next destination is 29km away, but an essential first stop in the park. The **Centro de Visitantes** (Visitors Centre; ☏922 63 35 76; Cruz del Carmen, Anaga Mountains; ⏱9.30am-4pm) has an exhibition centre and information on 13 walks, including several that start from here. There is also an excellent cafe and a small chapel.

❸ Picturesque Villages

Take the TF-136 to **Afur**. This beautiful tranquil hamlet has just 15 residents and is located deep in a lush ravine, complete with bubbling stream. Go to **La Cantina** (Afur, Anaga Mountains; ⏱10am-2pm & 5-7pm Mon-Sat) bar-cum-shop, a fascinating dusty clutter where elderly owner José Jimenez sells cheese, bread and local wine (€6 a bottle); try a glass for €1. Several walks are signposted from the carpark here.

❹ The Oldest Town

Back on the TF-12, follow the signs to **Taganana** on the TF-134; this steep winding road which eventually leads to the coast is one of the most stunning in the mountain range. Dating from the 16th century, Taganana is the largest and oldest town in the region. Explore the atmospheric cobbled streets and the 16th-century **Iglesia de Las Nieves**.

❺ Seafood & Cheese

Carry on to the blink-and-you-miss-it hamlet of **Benijo**, population around 20, and a recommended seafood restaurant, **El Fronton** (Benijo, Anaga Mountains; mains €7-9; ⏱10am-8pm); try the simple grilled fresh fish with *mojo* potatoes. Afterwards stroll up the hill to **Casa Paca**, a local producer of goat's cheese (stock up for €9 a kilo).

❻ Isolated Hamlet

Continue past El Draguillo where the road heads inland to **Charmorga**, another tiny hamlet nestled in a verdant palm-studded valley. Have a coffee at **Bar Casa Álvaro** (Charmorga, Anaga Mountains; snacks €3-6; ⏱10am-1.30pm & 5-7pm) and explore the streets lined with traditional houses with hipped Moorish-style tile roofs. Consider hiking the 1.3km trail to the abandoned village of **Tafada** signposted from here; the Cruz del Carmen visitors centre has a map.

❼ Fish Dinner

Return to San Andrés via the TF-123 and the TF-12. End your day with a seafood dinner at the **Confradía de Pescadores** (☏922 54 90 24; Avenida Marítimo de San Andrés; mains €10-18; ⏱Wed-Mon noon-11pm), which is owned by the local fishermen, so your seafood really *will* be as fresh as that day's catch.

The Best of
Tenerife

Tenerife's Best...

Auditorio de Tenerife (p34)
CALLE MONTES/GETTY IMAGES ©

Best
Eating

Tenerife's cuisine has moved on dramatically, even in the southern resorts where it used to be hard to find somewhere that didn't serve insipid 'international' cuisine. Today tourists can ditch the buffet in favour of more interesting fare, ranging from traditional Canarian cuisine, typified by robust homestyle cooking, right through to the haute cuisine of gastro temples, where innovative chefs serve some truly novel combinations.

DONHYPE/GETTY IMAGES ©

Dining Times & Customs

Breakfast *(desayuno)* is usually a no-nonsense affair with juice, coffee or tea, cereal or *gofio* (ground, roasted grain used in place of bread in Canarian cuisine), and toast with ham or cheese. *Churrerías* serve deliciously unhealthy deep-fried spiral-shaped churros (doughnuts), accompanied by a cup of hot chocolate, thick enough to stand a spoon up in.

The serious eating starts with lunch *(la comida)*. While locals tend to eat at home with the family, there's plenty of action at the restaurants too, starting at about 1pm and continuing until 4pm. In many restaurants a set-price *menú del día* is served at lunchtime.

Dinner is served late at home, generally from around 9pm, while restaurants will normally open at 8pm and serve until 11pm or later, especially in the tourist resorts. At-home dinners tend to be light for locals, but on weekends and special occasions they eat out with gusto and generally with the extended family.

Street Food

Street fare here is mainly restricted to churros (pictured) and *buñuelos* (doughnuts), though you'll also find kiosks selling fresh fruit juices like papaya and mango, if you've finally overdosed on the ice-cream.

☑ Top Tips

▶ Tap water is safe to drink, but you'll have to request it: most places offer bottled water. Ask for *un vaso de agua del grifo*.

▶ Bread will generally be provided (and added to your bill).

Best Traditional Cuisine

Bodeguita Canária A local Santa Cruz haunt serving freshly made Canarian classics in a homey setting. (p36)

La Llave de Las Nubes Tucked away and bypassed by tourists, this Santa Cruz restaurant is unwaveringly authentic. (p38)

La Casa de Oscar La Laguna's atmospheric,

packed La Casa serves up traditional, well-presented dishes. (p55)

Regulo A bastion of traditional cuisine in a fabulous Puerto de la Cruz historic mansion. (p72)

La Papaya Enduringly popular, this Puerto de la Cruz favourite serves simple Canarian classics. (p72)

La Tesela This no-frills place in La Orotava serves well-prepared local dishes. (p81)

Sabor Canario An atmospheric La Orotava restaurant with a traditional patio and authentic local cuisine. (p86)

Tapias La Bodega Elbow your way to this La Orotava bar to enjoy a medley of tapas or daily specials. (p86)

Tascafe Grimaldi Housed in a historic La Orotava mansion with a discerning menu of culinary classics. (p88)

Restaurante Fortuna Nova A good Puerto place to taste well-prepared authentic Spanish (and Canarian) dishes. (p98)

Best Contemporary Dining

El Aguarde Seasonally inspired dishes are an exquisite work of art; Santa Cruz. (p36)

Bulan In Santa Cruz, it draws a hip young crowd to its sumptuous surroundings and fashionable menu. (p38)

Guaydil Classy-but-casual La Laguna resto with a creative, international menu and contemporary decor. (p54)

The Oriental Monkey A hot dining option in Playa de las Américas with sizzling decor and an innovative fusion menu. (p109)

La Tasca de Bullicio Low-key fashionable place in La Orotava with a classy dining room and creative menu. (p88)

Best Authentic International

Capricho Libanés Lebanese-run La Laguna restaurant with freshly made Middle Eastern classics. (p57)

Le Bistrôt d'Alain Longstanding Los Cristianos favourite among Francophiles, showcasing classic French cuisine. (p97)

La Rosa di Bari An historic Puerto de la Cruz home with intimate dining spaces coupled with innovative *Italiano* cuisine. (p71)

Selma & Louisa Fresh simply prepared Swedish dishes, including baked goodies; Puerto de la Cruz. (p71)

Thai Botanico Exotic surroundings and a fragrant lightly spiced Asian cuisine; Playa de las Américas. (p109)

Christy's Unpretentious British grub in Costa Adeje, well cooked and authentic. (p110)

Worth a Trip

Overlooking terraced gardens with the sea in the distance, **Bodega el Reloj** (☎ 696 38 65 24; Camino Los Frontones 37; mains €12-15; ⏰ noon-4pm & 7-11pm Tue-Sun) has a beautiful setting with a touch of Italy's Amalfi Coast about it. The dishes are as good to look at as they are to eat and include steaks cooked on a hot stone. It's located around 3.5km southeast of La Orotava on the TF-21.

Best
Shopping

It's not hard to avoid straw donkeys and sex-on-the-beach shot glasses: Tenerife has a chain of quality-controlled souvenir shops that champion local art and crafts. The larger towns also have a pedestrian shopping area where idiosyncratic small shops jostle for space next to national chains. Delis are fun for browsing – *mojo* salsas make great gifts, as well as other gourmet goodies.

KRIS UBACH/GETTY IMAGES ©

Fashions & Textiles

While there are stores devoted to the main Spanish and international designers, you can also hunt out small boutiques with home-grown talent or specialising in ethnic or boho-chic threads. Shoes are generally a reliable buy here, good quality and generally cheaper than on the mainland. Leatherwear has also long been associated with Spain, and the Canaries have plenty of shops that sell jackets, bags and belts at highly competitive prices. Lace and embroidery are another speciality and the work is exquisite, although watch out for cheap imitations from China.

Ceramics & Jewellery

Simple terracotta pots that emulate Guanche designs are popular, along with more sophisticated ceramics and distinctive imported Spanish pottery. Silver jewellery and pearls are both relatively inexpensive. The company Tenerife Pearl advertises widely and has several outlets on the island.

Gourmet Goods

Gourmet food markets have opened in several towns and are fun, vibrant spaces where you can eat and drink, as well as shop. In addition there are small speciality stores where you can find an excellent range of jarred goodies as well as local cheese and *jamón* (ham; you can usually ask for a taste).

Best Fashion

Dolores Promesas This dynamic Santa Cruz–based designer appeals to the fashionably chic with her individual styles and richly patterned fabrics. (p42)

Carolina Boix Local shoe designer who specialises in comfortable inexpensive footwear for men and women; Santa Cruz. (p43)

El Ganso Head to this stylish boutique in the capital for punchy bright colours and innovative designs for men. (p43)

Carey Just the spot for picking up glitzy accessories or that show-stopping outfit; Puerto de la Cruz. (p75)

Tina A wonderfully eccentric Los Cristianos boutique; selling serious bling. (p95)

Sant Telmo Street in Puerto de la Cruz (p60)

Hensi Carries one of the widest local selections of shoes, concentrating on designer and national brands; Playa de las Américas. (p115)

Best Food Shops

El Rincon Extremeño A La Laguna temple to all things pork-inclined, particularly *jamón serrano* (Serrano ham), plus local cheese and gourmet goodies. (p59)

Licoreria Puerto A crammed-full space of every imaginable deli item, ranging from chilli-spiked sauces to chocolates; Puerto de la Cruz. (p75)

Olé Espacio Gourmet Seek out this Los Cristianos stall in the food market with its standout selection of cold cuts and cheese. (p101)

Best Souvenir Shops

Artenerife Top-quality art and crafts, including pottery and jewellery made by local artisans; Playa de las Américas. (p114)

Casa de la Aduana A large selection of arts and crafts, as well as wine and gourmet delights in Puerto de la Cruz. (p74)

MAIT Specialises in Latin American crafts displayed in a wonderful dazzle of patterns and colour; La Orotava. (p89)

La Alpizpa The original and colourful crafts here are made by locals with learning disabilities; Los Cristianos. (p100)

La Ranilla In a former fisherman's cottage in Puerto de la Cruz, this arty craft shop is ideal for unusual handmade gifts. (p74)

Best Bookshops

La Isla Bookshop A long-established well-stocked Santa Cruz bookshop on several floors; some English titles. (p43)

Librería Barbara A Los Cristianos-based multilingual Aladdin's cave of the written word with books, magazines, maps and more... (p100)

Best Vintage Stores

Dicky Morgan A super-stylish La Laguna store dedicated to vintage art, fashion and decor. (p59)

Vintage Store 13 This tantalising small space has some hidden gems among all the vintage jumble; Santa Cruz. (p42)

Best
Green Spaces

KAY MAERITZ/GETTY IMAGES ©

Tenerife has some truly lovely parks and green spaces, particularly around Puerto de la Cruz. The gardens here are truly diverse; some have a tangible sense of English gentility (with croquet lawns, no less), while others are more subtropical. Throughout the island the town parks are always family friendly, as well as being highly maintained and lushly landscaped with subtropical plants and the ubiquitous palms.

Pretty Parks

Like mainland Spain, parks and public gardens are an integral part of the infrastructure here and viewed as much-loved focal points for local life. There is always plenty of shady seating, as well as playgrounds and, increasingly, exercise equipment for adults. Generally toilets are also close to hand, as well as that other necessity: a cafe or bar. Some parks have bandstands where concerts take place, especially at fiesta time. Increasingly, parks are also showcasing sculpture, often contemporary, while others double as venues for art-and-craft markets.

Botanical Gardens

Tenerife is home to, arguably, the most stunning botanical gardens in the Canaries. They are wonderful places to while away a few hours, with the added plus of generally ensuring plenty of natural shade.

Anaga Parque Rural

One of the most impressive green spaces of Tenerife is the stunning unspoiled Anaga mountains, a rural natural park in the northeast of the island; note that you will need your own wheels in order to do this scenic corner of the island any justice. Make a day of it; there are some great picnic spots here, complete with barbecue pits and playgrounds.

Best City Parks

Parque García Sanabria A delightful collection of Mediterranean and subtropical trees and flowers, interspersed with water features and sculptures; Santa Cruz. (p31)

Plaza Príncipe de Asturias Sit under the shade of a giant Indian banyan tree at this fine capital-city park. (p30)

Best Botanical Gardens

Palmetum A vast collection of palms from around the world comprise this Santa Cruz park on the seafront. (p35)

Jardín Botánico The most famous gardens on Tenerife with a fascinating history and some extra-ordinary plants

Parque Marítimo César Manrique (p35)

and trees; Puerto de la Cruz. (p62)

Risco Belle Aquatic Gardens A lush water garden in Puerto de la Cruz with lakes, fountains and dazzling plants and flowers. (p63)

Sitio Litre Garden While orchids are the highlight here, the rest of this Puerto de la Cruz garden is a well-established leafy oasis of trickling water and tranquillity. (p68)

Hijuela del Botánico A delightful small botanical garden in La Orotava

with birds, butterflies and meandering pathways. (p86)

Jardínes del Marquesado de la Quinta Roja These terraced gardens provide a cascade of colour right in the centre of La Orotava. (p83)

Best for Families

Parque Marítimo César Manrique In the shadow of Santa Cruz' auditorium, clusters of palms give this Manrique-designed waterpark a welcome green feel. (p35)

Best Natural & Rural Parks

Anaga Mountains This northeasterly region is wild, unspoiled and very, very green with pine-clad mountains and forests of ancient laurels. (p122)

El Teide The terrain of El Teide is volcanic, rather than 'green' but is still full of colour and otherworldly intrigue; come here in springtime for a show of wildflowers. (p116)

Worth a Trip

Around 25km west of La Orotava, the stamp-size town of Icod de los Vinos is home to the **Drago Park** (adult/child €4/2.50; ☉9.30am-6.30pm), where you pay to get up close and personal with (apparently) the world's oldest and largest dragon tree. The park is also home to a pretty botanical garden and a so-called Guanche trail that includes a cave with disarmingly lifelike skulls and bones (great for scaring the tots!).

Best
For Free

Whether you're hitting the theme parks with the kids to burn off some energy or trawling the cultural hotspots and museums, having this much fun on holiday can seriously cost. The good news is that there are plenty of sights and experiences here that won't cost you a *céntimo*.

JOSÉ MIGUEL HERNÁNDEZ HERNÁNDEZ/GETTY IMAGES ©

Take a Walk

Some tourist offices offer free guided walks of the town, typically covering the main sights and, where appropriate, historic centre. Sometimes these have the added bonus of allowing you to peek into places normally closed to tourists. These walking tours are not always widely advertised, so be sure to check at the respective tourist office whether and when they are being offered. Occasionally there may be a minimal charge.

Free Days

There seems to be no hard-and-fast rule but many museums and sights have a free day a month (often the first Sunday), while others may have a time period during which there is no charge for visitors. Check their respective websites.

Best Free Art & Culture

Centro de Arte La Recova Themed, innovative exhibitions that showcase Spanish contemporary artists and photographers; Santa Cruz. (p36)

Sculpture Outdoor Pieces by some of the world's greatest sculptors can be seen in the park and around Santa Cruz. (p34)

Auditorio de Tenerife Have a free tour of this show-stopping great wave of an auditorium (pictured above) in the capital. (p34)

Best Flea Market

Rastro The largest flea market on the island, covering several streets in Santa Cruz and selling just about everything (including the kitchen sink). (p43)

Best Free Museums

Castillo de San Cristóbal Extraordinary historical underground museum in Santa Cruz. (p31)

Museo de Bellas Artes A superb Santa Cruz art gallery in a sumptuous setting with works by such smock-and-beret masters such as Brueghel and Ribera. (p34)

Casa del Vino La Baranda Learn all about wine production on the island at this little museum in El Sauzal. (p74)

Best
Drinking

Whether you are seeking a superb cup of coffee, a killer cocktail or just a long cold *cerveza* (beer) on a terrace bar, Tenerife has a multitude of choices. Terrace bars are probably where you'll spend a lot of your time and, with such an intoxicating combination of feel-good factors, what's not to like?

HEINRICH VAN DEN BERG/GETTY IMAGES ©

Choosing your Coffee...

What you need to know for your daily brew: *café con leche*: about 50% coffee, 50% hot milk; *sombra*: the same, but heavier on the milk; *café solo*: a short black coffee (or espresso); *cortado*: an expresso with a splash of milk; *cortado de leche y leche*: expresso made with condensed and normal milk.

Best Cafes

La Casita A charming small Santa Cruz cafe with old-world decor and gorgeous buttery cakes. (p31)

Coffee Break This fashionable arty space in La Laguna serves homemade pastries and savoury snacks. (p58)

Ebano Café Longstanding elegant cafe in Puerto de la Cruz with terrace seating and a relaxed vibe. (p73)

Best Cocktail Bars

Mojos y Mojitos Yep, the mojitos are pretty good at this animated bar in the centre of Santa Cruz. (p40)

Beach House A chic contemporary space near the Los Cristianos boardwalk for enjoying a long, cool cocktail. (p100)

Bar el Pincho Come here for some of the best seaviews at sunset from the sprawling terrace above the promenade in Playa de las Américas. (p113)

Papagayo Attracts a super-chic crowd with its stylish white-on-white decor and beachfront location in Playa de las Américas. (p112)

Best Local Bars

Bar 7 Vies This La Laguna bar is super popular with the local business bunch. (p57)

Bar Benidorm Traditional decor, Spanish ales on tap and a vibrant atmosphere make this a favourite La Laguna haunt. (p58)

Tasca Nano A Los Cristianos local with a choice of tapas and *raciones* to share. (p98)

Best Juice Bars

La Pera Limonera Interesting fruit-and-veg combos, plus other drinks (and wi-fi) make this a winner in La Laguna. (p58)

Bar Zumería Doña Papaya This simple no-frills place in the capital whisks up harvest-fresh fruit juices all day. (p40)

Best
Architecture

Tenerife is home to some of the most stunning historical architecture of the archipelago, with distinctive styles that are often combined to eye-catching effect. One of the most appealing features of the traditional building is the lavish ornamentation on the woodwork, visible in interior patios, on building facades and also evident on the painted Moorish-inspired Mudéjar (Islamic-influenced architecture) ceilings.

SANTIRF/GETTY IMAGES ©

Canarian Architecture

Influenced mainly by Portuguese and Andalusian traditional architecture, the typical Canarian house is distinctive for being practical, first and foremost. Rooms are typically built around a central patio, generally filled with flowers and water features, and ultimately designed to create an outdoor cool living space. More affluent homes will include a second-floor shaded gallery, usually constructed of carved wood and supported by slender stone or wood columns. The facades are typically painted in shades of yellow, pink and ochre. Latticed shutters allow air to circulate while providing shade from the sun, and door and window frames carved out of natural stone provide a classic elegance to the facade.

Religious Architecture

Many of Tenerife's churches and cathedrals date back to the 15th-century Gothic period while others include Renaissance elements, such as arches and cloisters, as well as baroque facades and entrances. Look out for the elaborate Mudéjar ceilings, which combine Christian art with Moorish patterns to stunning effect. The majority of churches here have simple whitewashed exteriors creating a distinctive island look and blending in well with their surroundings.

Best Contemporary Architecture

Auditorio de Tenerife A striking Santa Cruz building designed by Spain's leading contemporary architect, Santiago Calatrava. (p34)

Tenerife Espacio de las Artes (TEA) All angled lines, dramatic lighting and glass, the TEA interior is a thoroughly modern space in Santa Cruz. (p26)

Parque Marítimo César Manrique Manrique is the most famous architect in the Canaries; this Santa Cruz park provides a taster of his distinctive style. (p35)

Best Historical Architecture

Museo de Bellas Artes This neo-classical former convent in Santa Cruz is decorated with busts of famous people in Tenerife's history. (p34)

Centro de Arte La Recova A charming mid-19th-century building which was once home to the capital's market. (p36)

Teatro Guimerá A stunning art deco interior creates the perfect setting for highbrow entertainment in Santa Cruz. (p36)

Casa Torrehermosa A handsome 17th-century mansion in La Orotava with exceptional carved wooden detail. (p81)

Casa de los Capitanes This stately early 17th-century La Laguna building reflects the traditional Canarian architecture of the era. (p51)

Best Traditional Architecture

Casa de la Aduana This 17th-century former customs house in Puerto

de la Cruz is magnificent with its interior gallery and carved wood features. (p74)

Casa de los Balcones La Orotava's justifiably famous *casa*, with magnificent wooden balconies, ornate carved wood and galleried inner patio. (p78)

Casa del Turista A former La Orotava monastery dating from 1590, with most of the original features. (p85)

Casa Lercaro Built in La Laguna by an affluent family in the 16th century, with a picturesque inner terrace. (p48)

Liceo de Taoro This mid-19th-century neoclassical mansion in La Orotava has a stately presence. (p81)

Museo de las Alfombras Another sumptuous 16th-century mansion in La Orotava with most of the original features still in evidence. (p85)

Best Ecclesiastical Architecture

Iglesia de la Concepción An icon on the La Orotava skyline and a baroque beauty with distinctive twin towers. (p86)

Iglesia de Las Nieves This simple little church in the Anaga Mountains dates back to 1515 and is the fourth oldest on the island. (p122)

Iglesia de Nuestra Señora de la Concepción An exceptional Santa Cruz church dating from 1498, with a traditional Mudéjar coffered ceiling. (p34)

Catedral This imposing La Laguna cathedral (pictured left) exhibits several architectural styles, including neoclassical and Gothic. (p53)

Iglesia y ex-convento de San Agustín Have a peek at the fabulous cloisters at this evocative 17th-century ruined church in La Laguna. (p54)

Worth a Trip

Could the Canarios have had contact with America before Columbus famously sailed the ocean blue? If not, how to explain the Mayan-like **Pirámides de Güímar** (☏ 922 51 45 10; www.piramidesdeguimar.net; Calle Chacon, Güímar; adult/child €11/free; ☺9.30am-6pm)? The Norwegian scientist Thor Heyerdahl researched this question for many years, basing his theories on the pre-Columbian Mayan pyramids discovered in Güímar. Contemplate the mystery while visiting the restored ruins and museum in the east-coast village of Güímar.

Best
Walking

Many trails criss-cross the island, some are historic paths used before the days of cars and highways. The Parque Nacional del Teide and the Anaga Mountains, in particular, offer a variety of hikes, ranging from easy walks to adrenalin-charged volcanic or mountain climbs. The beachside promenades are also great for strolling. Keen walkers should avoid the peak summer heat of July and August.

MARIDAV/GETTY IMAGES ©

Best Urban Strolls

Puerto de la Cruz It's a gentle incline but a pleasant walk, heading from the centre to Puerto's gardens, via the Mirador de la Paz. (p60)

La Laguna Tenerife's most ideal (and picturesque town) to explore on foot with no hills and spellbinding architecture. (p46)

Santa Cruz de Tenerife Pick up the map from the tourist office that maps out the city-centre sculpture walk. (p22)

Hiking Trails

La Orotava The lush valley surrounding the town has a maze of footpaths through spectacular scenery. (p76)

Garachico Just outside the town you can hike trails that follow the path of the former lava flows. (p118)

El Teide There are over 20 well-signposted trails you can follow around the volcano. (p116)

Aguamansa Walk through ancient forests of laurel trees and pines high in the mountains near La Orotava. (p87)

Anaga Mountains Head for the Cruz del Carmen visitors centre, the starting point for several great walks. (p122)

Best Promenades

Costa Adeje Take a bracing stroll eastwards along the seafront promenade from Playa del Duque to La Caleta. (p102)

El Médano You can walk around 3km along the promenade here; the tourist office also has a map of local walks. (p93)

Santa Cruz de Tenerife The revamped waterfront promenade here equals a pleasant walk eastwards from the port. (p22)

Los Cristianos Harbour It's a gentle stroll along the beachfront and down to the harbour, and very pretty at sunset time. (p90)

Best Trekking Companies

Trekking Tenerife (www.trekking-tenerife.com) Organises several treks of varying distances and levels of difficulty on Tenerife and other islands.

Best
Beaches

Tenerife has some superb beaches which, unlike other islands here, are not restricted to black volcanic sand (although there are some here, as well). Beaches come in every shape and size – long and golden, intimate and calm, action packed and windy and wavy. Year-round sun and warm water (18°C to 26°C) makes the appeal of the beaches a no-brainer for most folk.

Beach Access for All

Tenerife is arguably the most accessible Canary Island destination for anyone with mobility problems, and the beaches are no exception, particularly in the south where Los Cristianos probably leads the way with beach terraces specifically geared towards wheelchairs or mobility issues. Amphibious chairs are also available here, as well as Red Cross staff who can offer extra assistance and advice.

Source of Sand

It is no secret that Tenerife is volcanic and that those golden sandy beaches that you see here (and other Canary Island resorts) are not historically inherent, but a result of a considerable investment by the tourism authorities – with a little European Community help. In some cases, sand has been pumped from the seabed; in others, it's been imported from the Sahara Desert.

Best Golden Sands

Playa de Las Teresitas
Located near Santa Cruz, this fine beach (pictured above) is untainted by tourism and has a beautiful setting. (p36)

Playa de las Vistas
A sublime beach with fine golden sand, linking Los Cristianos with Playa de las Américas. (p106)

Playa del Duque
Appropriately named 'the Duke's beach' with a more exclusive feel than some sandy stretches. (p106)

Best for Watersports

Los Cristanos The fishing port here is lined with kiosks offering a wide range of water bound trips and tours. (p92)

El Médano One of the best beaches on the island for wind- and kite-surfing with beachside operators offering courses. (p93)

Playa Honda One of the region's top surfing schools is conveniently located on this central beach in Playa de las Américas. (p106)

Best
For Kids

CULTURA TRAVEL/JIBACH/DE LA RIVA/GETTY IMAGES ©

Tenerife has to be one of the most family-friendly destinations this side of Disneyland. Stripped back to basics, the beaches and virtual year-round sunshine are pretty good raw ingredients, and then there are the theme parks, camel rides, museums, parks and watersports. The culture here also celebrates children, who will be made welcome just about everywhere, including restaurants and bars.

For Free

While there are plenty of attractions designed specifically with children in mind, including theme parks and zoos, public spaces – such as town and village plazas – also morph into informal play-grounds with children kicking a ball around, riding bikes and playing, while parents enjoy a drink and tapa at one of the surrounding bars. Local children also stay up late and at fiestas it's commonplace to see even tiny ones toddling the streets at 2am.

Accommodation

Most of the mid- and upper-range hotels can also arrange babysitting. Also, provided you are willing to share a bed with your tot, many hotels here do not impose a surcharge, although requesting a cot or extra bed will normally up the price slightly.

What to Bring

Although you may want to bring a small supply of items you are used to having back home (particularly baby products), Tenerife is likely to have everything you will need. Even in an emergency situation (ie running out of nappies!), there will always be one pharmacy that remains open 24-hours nearby, wherever you are staying on the island.

For further information about travelling with children, check out www.lonelyplanet.com/family-travel, www.travelwithyourkids.com and www.family travelnetwork.com.

☑ Top Tips

▶ Always check ask at the tourist office for a list of family activities, including the location of playgrounds and the dates of traditional fiestas (there's many, and they usually involve parades and bouncy castles!).

▶ Make sure your kids take a siesta if possible, otherwise they may miss out on the evening action.

Best Attractions

Parque Marítimo César Manrique A vast watery playground in Santa Cruz with several pools, including those with shallow depths for toddlers. (p35)

Lago Martiánez Another Manrique creation, geared towards families and splashing kids, in Puerto de la Cruz. (p69)

Observatorio del Teide Older children will get a kick out of having a chance to stargaze through the mammoth telescope in Parque Nacional del Teide. (p118)

Roques de García The gentle walk in Parque Nacional del Teide from the carpark to these extraordinary rock formations is suitable for strollers. (p117)

Best Museums

Museo de la Naturaleza y el Hombre The exhibits of reptiles, birds and, in particular, bugs should fascinate children of all ages; Santa Cruz. (p24)

Museo Militar de Almeyda In the capital; older bloodthirsty kids may like gazing at the cannon that blew off Nelson's arm! (p36)

Museo de la Historia de Tenerife Kids may want to bypass the main exhibits and head straight for the fairytale carriages out back; La Laguna. (p48)

Museo de la Ciencia y el Cosmos Fascinating science museum in La Laguna with exhibits geared towards children of all ages. (p54)

Watersports

Neptuno Dolphin-spotting usually goes down well with kids of all ages; Los Cristianos. (p109)

Travelin' Lady This Los Cristianos outfit organises longer boat trips with whale watching (and food). (p97)

Club de Buceo An excellent Los Cristianos diving company, which offers bubblemaker courses for kids. (p97)

Worth a Trip

A watery wonderland with an intriguing Thai theme, **Siam Park** (902 06 00 00; www.siampark.net; Autopista Sur exit 28; adult/child €34/23; 10am-6pm) is the newest attraction in the south and covers a vast 14 hectares. Rides range from the near-vertical Tower of Power (pictured left) to the Lost City: an adventure playground for tots with mini-slides, fountains and pools.

Best Sports & Activities

True: if it's the height of summer, you may not feel like shifting far from the (beach) bar stool or sunbed but, at other times, it's good to know that there are plenty of activities available, ranging from the obvious gentle breaststroke in the sea to those that involve a backpack with muesli bars and several litres of water.

KAY MAERITZ / LOOK FOTO/GETTY IMAGES ©

On Land

When you are virtually guaranteed perfect weather for twelve months of the year, you need to be out in the open. Hiking or walking is the most popular activity here and there is plenty of choice ranging from gentle seafront strolls to adrenalin-fuelled hikes. Alternatively, there are several world-class golf courses; book a game through www.tenerife golfteetimes.com. Beaches in the larger resorts generally have a volleyball net and a game going on, while tennis clubs are increasing in numbers; check out www.tenislasamericas.com if you're staying in the south. Throughout the resorts, the seafront is a fine setting for a jog or a spin, with the norm of a bike lane separate from traffic and pedestrians.

Best Watersports

Travelin' Lady A long-standing and reputable Los Cristianos boat-tour operator, which specialises in whalewatching tours. (p97)

K-16 Surf You can rent a board or take a class (or both) at this serious surf-dude school in Playa de las Américas. (p107)

Arona Tenerife Surf Academy Another reputable Playa de las Américas outfit for perfecting those on-board skills. (p106)

Aqua Marina This Playa de las Américas operator has a vast range of diving courses, including try dives for absolute beginners. (p106)

Club de Buceo A long-standing Los Cristianos diving school that covers the gamut of courses including bubblemaker lessons for kids. (p97)

Neptuno Plenty of boat-tour choices with this Los Cristianos outfit, including one with food, drink and whale spotting. (p109)

El Cardumen As well as diving, this outfit in Puerto de la Cruz offers paragliding. (p70)

Best Spas

Mare Nostrum Pamper yourself with a spa treatment at this luxurious marble-clad spa in Playa de las Américas. (p106)

Hotel Botánico This spa centre (pictured) in Puerto de la Cruz has fabulous Thai decor and offers a range of treatments, including aromatherapy massage. (p145)

Best
Museums & Art

VIEW PICTURES/CONTRIBUTOR/GETTY IMAGES ©

After decades under the dictatorship of General Franco, art and culture now have a very real presence in Tenerife and museums throughout the island showcase local works of art, as well as history, archaeology, crafts and other aspects of the lifestyle and culture here. Museums are often located in stunning historical buildings that can be just as fascinating as the exhibits.

Best Art Galleries

Tenerife Espacio de las Artes (TEA) World-class contemporary art museum designed by Herzog & De Meuron and Virgilio Gutiérrez (pictured) in Santa Cruz, showcasing local surrealist master Óscar Domínguez. (p26)

Museo de Bellas Artes A former Santa Cruz convent houses this collection of fine masters from the Flemish and Spanish schools. (p34)

Fundación Cristino de Vera This delightful small gallery in La Laguna is dedicated to the work of the late local artist Cristino de Vera. (p53)

Museo de Arte Contemporáneo This Puerto de la Cruz collection includes fine works by artists in the calibre of Picasso and Dalí. (p68)

Best Museums

Museo de la Naturaleza y el Hombre A cracking museum in the capital with exhibits ranging from archaeology to butterflies and birds. (p24)

Museo de la Historia de Tenerife An eclectic collection of exhibits housed in a fittingly period building in La Laguna. (p48)

Museo de la Ciencia y el Cosmos Great science museum in La Laguna for kids of all ages with plenty of hands-on exhibits and displays. (p54)

Museo de Artesania Iberoamericana This La Orotava museum takes a look at the fascinating link between the Canarias and the Americas. (p83)

Museo Arqueológico Well laid-out displays chronicle the history of

the island from the time of the Guanches; Puerto de la Cruz. (p69)

Casa del Vino La Baranda Learn everything you need to know about local wine production, including the tasting; El Sauzal. (p74)

Casa de los Balcones This small folkloric museum in La Orotava has rooms furnished in typical 17th-century style. (p78)

Museo de las Alfombras Discover the background and process behind those fabulous floral Corpus Christi displays in La Orotava. (p85)

Convento de San Francisco Exhibits here range from archaeology to modern sculpture, exhibited in the cloisters of Garachico's beautiful former convent. (p121)

Survival Guide

Survival Guide

Before You Go

When to Go

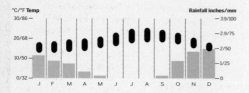

°C/°F Temp
30/86 —
20/68 —
10/50 —
0/32 —

Rainfall inches/mm
— 3.9/100
— 2.9/75
— 2/50
— 1/25
— 0

J F M A M J J A S O N D

➡ Winter (Dec–Feb)
Pleasantly warm, except on El Teide where deep winter can see snowfall closing the mountain.

➡ Spring (Mar–Apr)
Surfers will find the best waves in March; good for hiking and wildflowers.

➡ Summer (May–Sep)
Expect 11 hours of daily sunshine with an average of 28°C in August; a few degrees cooler during the surrounding months.

➡ Autumn (Oct–Nov)
Ideal temperatures around the 21°C mark and there's fewer tourists; some hotels may drop their prices slightly.

Book Your Stay

☑ **Top Tip** Some hotels still charge a costly amount for internet access, although it should be free these days. Always check when you book as it can up your hotel bill considerably.

Useful Websites

Casas Rurales (www.ecoturismocanarias.com) Has an extensive selection of rural accommodation throughout the island.

Lonely Planet (www.lonelyplanet.com) Author-recommended reviews and online booking.

Tenerife Holiday Apartments (www.tha-tenerife.co.uk) Over 150 apartments and villas available for holiday rental.

Country Houses (www.ruraltenerife.net) Rural cottages and traditional Canarian country houses for rent.

Best Budget

Hotel Adonis Capital
(Santa Cruz; www.adonis
resorts.com) Rooms are
well equipped and
spacious.

**Bed & Breakfast La
Laguna** (La Laguna; www.
bblalaguna.com) A B&B-
cum-hostel with brightly
painted rooms and a
pretty patio.

Hotel Sun Holidays
(Puerto de la Cruz; www.hotel
sunholidays.com) Superbly
equipped rooms plus a
lovely rooftop terrace.

Hotel Andrea's (Los
Cristianos; www.hotelandreas.
com) Small neat hotel with
comfy communal sitting
room with TV.

Hotel Reveron Plaza
(Los Cristianos; www.hoteles
reveron.com) Oldest hotel
in Los Cristianos; tradi-
tionally furnished and
family run.

Best Midrange

Hotel Contemporáneo
(Santa Cruz; ☎922 77 02 00)
Delightful rural hotel and
restaurant.

Hotel Taburiente (Santa
Cruz; www.hoteltaburien
te.com) Contemporary-
style hotel; ask for a room

with a balcony overlook-
ing the park.

Hotel Aguere (La
Laguna; www.hotelaguere.
es) Friendly historic hotel
with stunning glassed-in
central patio.

Hotel Monopol (Puerto de
la Cruz; www.monopol
tf.com) Beautiful 18th-
century building houses
this grande dame of a
hotel.

Hotel La Quinta Roja
(Garachico; www.quinta
roja.com) Restored 16th-
century manor house
with rooms set around a
gracious patio.

Best Top End

**Hotel-Apartamentos
Nivaria** (La Laguna; www.
hotelnivaria.com) Former
home of a marquis with
elegant rooms, plus a spa
and gym.

Hotel Tigaiga (Puerto de
la Cruz; www.tigaiga.com)
Family run with contem-
porary, bright and airy
rooms and suites.

Hotel Botánico (Puerto de
la Cruz; www.hotelbotanico.
com) Long-established
hotel with an exclusive
spa and lush tropical
gardens.

**Parador de Las Cañadas
del Teide** (El Teide; www.
parador.es) Located in
the heart of the national
park, rooms are rustically
styled and comfortable.

Arriving in Tenerife

➔ Two airports serve the
island of Tenerife.

➔ **Tenerife Norte** (Los
Rodeos; ☎922 63 56 35;
www.aena.es) is the older
and smaller of the two, located on the outskirts of
the capital of Santa Cruz
de Tenerife. Although relatively small, it has good
facilities including an
exchange booth, several
car-rental agencies, a bar
and a helpful information
booth (8am to 7pm).

➔ The flashier **Tenerife
Sur** (Reina Sofía; ☎922 75
95 10; www.aena.es) is located around 20km east
of Playa de las Ámericas
and handles international
flights.

From Tenerife Sur
Airport

➔ Bus 343 goes to Playa
de las Américas and

Los Cristianos (one-way €3.70, 45 minutes) roughly every 40 minutes from 8.25am to 11pm, continuing to Tenerife Norte airport (€9.70, 50 minutes) from 8.25am to 11pm daily.

➡ A taxi from Tenerife Sur to the centre of Los Cristianos and Playa de las Ámericas will cost around €26 and €28 respectively.

From Tenerife Norte Airport

➡ Bus 102 goes to Santa Cruz de Tenerife roughly every 30 minutes from 12.30am to 11.30pm (one-way €2.65, 20 minutes), continuing to La Laguna (€2.45) and Puerto de la Cruz (€4.75). The express bus 343 goes to Tenerife Sur airport (€9.70, 50 minutes) roughly every hour from 7am to 9.45pm daily.

➡ A taxi from Tenerife Norte to the centre of Santa Cruz will cost around €20. A ride to the Tenerife Sur airport will cost around €70.

Getting Around

Bicycle

☑ **Best for...** The obvious! Wind in the hair, building up those calf muscles and enjoying the freedom to explore at exactly your own pace.

➡ Cycling around Tenerife is an extremely pleasant way to see the island and you can rent mountain and city bikes at all the main resorts and larger towns. Expect to pay a

minimum of €12 a day with a standard deposit of around €50.

➡ Be wary on the roads. Bicycle lanes in the urban environment are sadly minimal, although beachside boulevards are increasingly incorporating space for bike riding. Drivers are not always as courteous as you would like.

Bus

☑ **Best for...** Travelling on a budget. The bus line is very inexpensive especially on the longer routes.

➡ The first thing you should know about the buses here is their Canarian name: *guagua* (pronounced 'wa-wa'), although if you ask about *autobuses*, you will still be understood. Aside from Santa Cruz, services in most towns and even resorts do not operate out of a dedicated bus station, but a street with a kiosk where you can purchase tickets and pick up a bus timetable.

➡ Buses are operated by **TITSA** (Transportes Interurbanos de Tenerife SA; www.titsa.com) and cover the entire island. The bus service is fast, comfortable and inexpensive.

Dos & Don'ts

Eating & Drinking It is customary to keep your cutlery between meals, unless you are in a top-end restaurant.

Visiting Churches Never take photos in a church when a service is taking place.

Greetings Locals generally greet friends and strangers alike with a kiss on both cheeks, although males generally shake hands instead.

The website, in English and Spanish, includes a comprehensive list of routes and times.

Car

☑ **Best for...** Getting off the beaten track; car rental is the only option if you want to get away from the main tourist resorts and really explore the island.

➡ Renting a car in Tenerife is highly recommended; the bus service is good but restricts you time-wise and exploring inland is only really possible with your own wheels.

➡ All the major international car-rental companies are represented in Tenerife and there are also plenty of local operators.

➡ To rent a car you need to have a driver's licence, be aged 21 or over and have a credit or debit card; prices start from around €20 per day.

➡ Speed limits are 120km on motorways, 100km on dual highways, 90km on country roads, 50km in built-up areas and 20km in residential zones.

➡ Generally you can't take a hire car from one island to another. Cicar (www.cicar.com), a Canary Islands company, is an exception as they have offices located throughout the archipelago.

➡ Rent your car online before you travel, to both save money and also avoid being in a situation where there are no available cars for rental (it can happen in high season).

➡ Third-party motor insurance is a minimum requirement when renting a car in Tenerife.

➡ Unless you are intending to settle in Tenerife, there is no advantage whatsoever in bringing your own vehicle.

➡ *Gasolina* (petrol) is much cheaper in Tenerife than elsewhere in Spain because it is not taxed as heavily. *Sin plomo* (unleaded) and *diesel* (diesel) petrol are available everywhere with generally two grades on offer for each.

Taxi

☑ **Best for...** Convenience

➡ Always use official, and easily identifiable, taxis at the airport.

➡ If you can't locate your hotel, ask a local taxi to lead you there.

Tram

☑ **Best for...** The tram is by far the most convenient mode of travel between between Santa Cruz and La Laguna, due primarily to its frequency: every 12 minutes.

➡ Tranvía de Tenerife (www.metrotenerife.com) is the most enjoyable and comfortable way to travel between Santa Cruz and La Laguna. There are two lines. The main line, Line 1, is 12.5km long with 21 stops and connects with Line 2, which is 3.6km long and has 6 stops, two of which are transfer stops. Most visitors will take Line 1, however, which connects Santa Cruz with Avenida de la Trinidad (a five-minute walk from the historic centre of La Laguna).

➡ Tickets are bought from a machine and cost €1.35 for a single ride, €6 for five trips and €45 for a month pass; note that you cannot buy tickets on the tram.

➡ Trams run from 6am to midnight daily and the journey from Santa Cruz to La Laguna takes around 35 minutes.

➡ Don't forget to punch your ticket in the machine when you get on the tram, as failure to do so can result in a €100 fine.

Essential Information

Business Hours

☑ **Top Tip** In Tenerife's non-resort towns, shops typically close from around 1.30pm to 5pm while locals take time out to have a siesta.

Reviews in this guidebook list the standard opening hours for high season; hours tend to decrease outside that time. General standard opening hours:

Banks 8.30am–2pm Monday to Friday

Bars 7pm to midnight

Post Offices 8.30am to 8.30pm Monday to Friday, 9.30am to 1pm Saturday (large cities); 8.30am to 2.30pm Monday to Friday, 9.30am to 1pm Saturday (elsewhere)

Restaurants Meals served 1pm to 4pm and 8pm to late (earlier opening hours in the southern resorts)

Shops 10am to 2pm and 5pm to 9pm Monday to Friday, 10am to 2pm Saturday

Supermarkets 9am to 9pm Monday to Friday

Discount Cards

☑ **Top Tip** To receive any discount, photo ID is essential.

➡ Reduced prices usually apply for seniors over 60 or 65 (depending on the place) at various museums and attractions and occasionally on transport.

➡ Students typically get a discount of about half the normal fee, though not everywhere.

Electricity

220V/50Hz

Emergency

Ambulance (☎061)

EU standard Emergency number (☎112)

Fire Brigade (Bomberos; ☎080)

National Police (☎062)

Local Police (☎092)

Money

Currency Euro (€)

ATMs Widely available; there's usually a charge on ATM cash withdrawals abroad.

Moneychangers Located at the airports and in the major resorts. Offer longer opening hours than banks but, generally, worse exchange rates.

Cash Banks and building societies offer the best rates; take your passport.

Credit cards Accepted in most hotels, restaurants and shops; you may need to show passport or other photo ID.

Tipping Small change in restaurants; round up to the nearest euro in taxis.

Public Holidays

Many shops are closed and many attractions operate on reduced hours on the following dates:

Año Nuevo (New Year's Day) 1 January

Día de los Reyes Magos
(Three Kings Day)
6 January

Viernes Santo (Good
Friday) March/April

Fiesta del Trabajo
(Labour Day) 1 May

**La Asunción de la
Virgen** (Feast of the
Assumption) 15 August

Día de la Hispanidad
(National Day)
12 October

Todos los Santos (All
Saints' Day) 1 November

**La Inmaculada Con-
cepción** (Feast of the
Immaculate Conception)
8 December

Navidad (Christmas)
25 December

In addition, the regional
government sets a fur-
ther five holidays, while
local councils allocate
another two. Common
holidays include the
following:

Martes de Carnival
(Carnival Tuesday)
February/March

Día de San Juan (St
John's Day) 19 March

Jueves Santo (Maundy
Thursday) March/April

Money-Saving Tips

➡ Look out for free entry at sights, often the first
Sunday of the month.

➡ Order the *menú del día* for lunch in restaurants.

➡ Request tap water *(un vaso de agua del grifo)*
rather than the over-priced bottled variety.

**Día de las Islas
Canarias** (Canary
Islands Day) 30 May

Corpus Christi (the
Thursday after the eighth
Sunday after Easter
Sunday) June

Día de Santiago Apóstol
(Feast of St James the
Apostle, Spain's patron
saint) 25 July. In Santa
Cruz de Tenerife the day
also marks the commem-
oration of the defence of
the city against British
Admiral Nelson.

Día de la Constitución
(Constitution Day)
6 December

Safe Travel

☑ **Top Tip** If you are
unfortunate enough to
be robbed, ensure that
you report it to the police
within 24 hours or your
insurance may be void.

➡ Always make sure valu-
ables are out of sight in
your car.

➡ Politely refuse to fill out
any scratch cards on the
street; most will lead to a
timeshare scam.

➡ Check your bills in
restaurants to ensure
you haven't been over-
charged.

➡ Watch your wallet,
particularly in crowded
places like street markets.

Telephone

Mobile Phones Local
SIM cards are widely
available and can be
used in European and
Australian mobile phones.
Other phones may need
to be set to roaming but
be wary of additional
charges.

**Phone Codes
International access
code** (☎00)

Canary Islands code
(☎34; same as Spain)

**National toll-free
number** (☎900)

Toilets

There are very few public toilets on the island. The easiest option is to wander into a bar or cafe and use its facilities. The polite thing to do is to have a coffee or the like before or after, but you're unlikely to raise too many eyebrows if you don't. Alternatively, if you feel awkward but don't fancy a drink, you can offer, say, 0.50c which will be appreciated although generally declined. This said, some curmudgeonly places in popular tourist areas post notices saying that their toilets are for customers only.

Tourist Information

The **Oficina de Turismo** (www.todotenerife.es) has offices in the main towns and resorts throughout the island.

Santa Cruz de Tenerife (Map p32, D3; ☎ 922 23 95 92; www.todotenerife.es; Plaza España; ⏰ 9am-6pm Mon-Fri, 9.30am-1.30pm Sat)

Puerto de la Cruz (Map p66; ☎ 922 38 60 00; www. todotenerife.es; Casa de la Aduana, Calle Lonjas; ⏰ 9am-8pm Mon-Fri, to 5pm Sat & Sun)

La Laguna (Map p52; ☎ 922 63 11 94; www. todotenerife.es; Calle Carrera 7; ⏰ 9am-8pm Mon-Fri, to 2pm Sat & Sun)

La Orotava (Map p82; ☎ 922 32 30 41; www. todotenerife.es; Calle Calvario 4; ⏰ 9am-5pm Mon-Fri)

Los Cristianos (Map p96; ☎ 922 75 71 37; www.arona. org; Centro Cultural, Plaza Pescador 1)

Playa de las Américas (Map p104; ☎ 922 79 76 68; Centro Comercial City Center, Avenida Rafael Puig Lluvina)

Travellers with Disabilities

➡ Most hotels and an increasing number of restaurants have wheelchair access.

➡ All buses and the tram line are wheelchair accessible.

➡ Some museums have Braille in the lifts.

➡ Resorts in the south have excellent facilities overall, including amphibious chairs.

Mobility Abroad (www. mobilityabroad.com) A longstanding international company that rents out mobility scooters with outlets in Tenerife.

Accessible Travel & Leisure (www.access ibletravel.co.uk) Claims to be the biggest UK travel agent dealing with travel for the disabled, and encourages the disabled to travel independently.

Visas

EU & Schengen Countries No visa required.

Australia, Canada, Israel, Japan, New Zealand and the USA No visa required for tourist visits of up to 90 days.

Other Countries Check with a Spanish embassy or consulate.

➡ To work or study in Tenerife a special visa may be required: contact a Spanish embassy or consulate before travel.

Language

Spanish (*español*) – often referred to as *castellano* (Castilian) to distinguish it from other languages spoken in Spain – is the language of Tenerife. While you'll find an increasing number of locals who speak some English, don't count on it. Travellers who learn a little Spanish will be amply rewarded as Spaniards appreciate the effort, no matter how basic your understanding of the language.

Most Spanish sounds are pronounced the same as their English counterparts. Those familiar with Spanish might notice the Andalusian or even Latin American lilt of the Canarian accent – 'll' is pronounced as y and the 'lisp' you might expect with 'z' and 'c' before vowels sounds more like s while the letter 's' itself is hardly pronounced at all. If you follow our coloured pronunciation guides (with the stressed syllables in italics) you'll be understood just fine. Note that 'm/f' indicates masculine and feminine forms.

To enhance your trip with a phrasebook, visit **lonelyplanet.com**.

Basics

Hello.
Hola.   o·la

Goodbye.
Adiós.   a·dyos

How are you?
¿Qué tal?   ke tal

Fine, thanks.
Bien, gracias.   byen gra·syas

Please.
Por favor.   por fa·vor

Thank you.
Gracias.   gra·syas

Excuse me.
Perdón.   per·don

Sorry.
Lo siento.   lo syen·to

Yes./No.
Sí./No.   see/no

Do you speak (English)?
¿Habla (inglés)?   a·bla (een·gles)

I (don't) understand.
Yo (no) entiendo.   yo (no) en·tyen·do

What's your name?
¿Cómo se   ko·mo se
llama?   lya·ma

My name is ...
Me llamo ...   me lya·mo ...

Eating & Drinking

What would you recommend?
¿Qué   ke
recomienda?   re·ko·myen·da

Cheers!
¡Salud!   sa·loo

That was delicious!
¡Estaba   es·ta·ba
buenísimo!   bwe·nee·see·mo

The bill, please.
La cuenta,   la kwen·ta
por favor.   por fa·vor

I'd like ...
Quisiera ...   kee·sye·ra ...

a coffee	un café	oon ka·fe
a table for two	una mesa para dos	oo·na me·sa pa·ra dos
two beers	dos cervezas	dos ser·ve·sas

Shopping

I'd like to buy ...
Quisiera kee·sye·ra
comprar ... kom·prar ...

Can I look at it?
¿Puedo verlo? pwe·do ver·lo

How much is it?
¿Cuánto cuesta? kwan·to kwes·ta

That's very expensive.
Es muy caro. es mooy ka·ro

Can you lower the price?
¿Podría bajar po·dree·a ba·khar
un poco oon po·ko
el precio? el pre·syo

I'm just looking.
Sólo estoy so·lo es·toy
mirando. mee·ran·do

Emergencies

Help!
¡Socorro! so·ko·ro

Call a doctor!
¡Llame a lya·me a oon
un médico! me·dee·ko

Call the police!
¡Llame a lya·me a
la policía! la po·lee·see·a

I'm lost. (m/f)
Estoy perdido/a. es·toy per·dee·do/a

I'm ill. (m/f)
Estoy enfermo/a. es·toy en·fer·mo/a

Time & Numbers

What time is it?
¿Qué hora es? ke o·ra es

It's (10) o'clock.
Son (las diez). son (las dyes)

morning	*mañana*	ma·nya·na
afternoon	*tarde*	tar·de
evening	*noche*	no·che

yesterday	*ayer*	a·yer
today	*hoy*	oy
tomorrow	*mañana*	ma·nya·na

1	*uno*	oo·no
2	*dos*	dos
3	*tres*	tres
4	*cuatro*	kwa·tro
5	*cinco*	seen·ko
6	*seis*	seys
7	*siete*	sye·te
8	*ocho*	o·cho
9	*nueve*	nwe·ve
10	*diez*	dyes

Transport & Directions

Where's ...?
¿Dónde está ...? don·de es·ta ...

Where's the station?
¿Dónde está don·de es·ta
la estación? la es·ta·syon

What's the address?
¿Cuál es la kwal es la
dirección? dee·rek·syon

Can you show me (on the map)?
¿Me lo puede me lo pwe·de
indicar een·dee·kar
(en el mapa)? (en el ma·pa)

I want to go to ...
Quisiera ir a ... kee·sye·ra eer a ...

What time does it arrive/leave?
¿A qué hora a ke o·ra
llega/sale? lye·ga/sa·le

Please tell me when we get to ...
¿Puede avisarme pwe·de a·vee·sar·me
cuando lleguemos kwan·do ye·ge·mos
a ...? a ...

I want to get off here.
Quiero bajarme kye·ro ba·khar·me
aquí. a·kee

Behind the Scenes

Send Us Your Feedback

We love to hear from travellers – your comments help make our books better. We read every word, and we guarantee that your feedback goes straight to the authors. Visit **lonelyplanet.com/contact** to submit your updates and suggestions.

Note: We may edit, reproduce and incorporate your comments in Lonely Planet products such as guidebooks, websites and digital products, so let us know if you don't want your comments reproduced or your name acknowledged. For a copy of our privacy policy visit lonelyplanet.com/privacy.

Josephine's Thanks

I would like to thank all the helpful folk at the various tourist information offices, as well as Jorge Gonzalez, a valuable contact in Tenerife. Thanks too to destination editor Lorna Parkes and to all those involved in the title from the Lonely Planet offices, as well as to all my Spanish *malagueño* friends who provided endless advice, contacts and tips, and to Robin Chapman for looking after Marilyn (the cat).

Acknowledgments

Cover photograph: La Orotava, Puerto de la Cruz and El Teide; Olimpio Fantuz/4Corners.

This Book

This 1st edition of Lonely Planet's *Pocket Tenerife* guidebook was researched and written by Josephine Quintero. This guidebook was produced by the following:

Destination Editor Lorna Parkes **Product Editors** Kate Kiely, Amanda Williamson **Regional Senior Cartographer** Anthony Phelan **Book Designer** Virginia Moreno **Cartographer** Julie Sheridan **Assisting Editors** Jodie Lea Martire, Rosie Nicholson **Assisting Book Designer** Cam Ashley **Cover Researcher** Campbell McKenzie **Thanks to** Sasha Baskett, Jo Cooke, Victoria Harrison, Andi Jones, Karyn Noble, Alison Ridgway, Angela Tinson, Tony Wheeler

Index

See also separate subindexes for:

⊗ **Eating** p156

☺ **Drinking** p157

☆ **Entertainment** p157

🔒 **Shopping** p157

Our Writer

Josephine Quintero

Spain is Josephine's favourite country on earth and she has lived on the mainland for over 20 years. She has visited Tenerife on numerous happy occasions and co-authored three editions of Lonely Planet's *Canary Islands* guide, as well as numerous other LP titles. Josephine always packs her hiking boots to stride out on El Teide, but still comes back several kilos heavier, thanks to those addictive *mojo* potatoes. Highlights during this trip included gazing at evocative art at the TEA museum in Santa Cruz and discovering tiny hamlets in the Anaga Mountains where there were more goats than folk. She was swept up in the traditional Sunday pilgrimage to Candelaria's basilica and swept off her feet with the live Latino music in Puerto. Read more about Josephine at lonelyplanet.com/members/josephinequintero.

Published by Lonely Planet Publications Pty Ltd
ABN 36 005 607 983
1st edition – Feb 2016
ISBN 978 1 74360 703 9
© Lonely Planet 2016   Photographs © as indicated 2016
10 9 8 7 6 5 4 3
Printed in Malaysia

Although the authors and Lonely Planet have taken all reasonable care in preparing this book, we make no warranty about the accuracy or completeness of its content and, to the maximum extent permitted, disclaim all liability arising from its use.